panchang

moon astrology

panchang
moon astrology

how to do the right thing at the right time

michael geary

Thorsons

Thorsons
An Imprint of HarperCollins*Publishers*
77–85 Fulham Palace Road
Hammersmith, London W6 8JB

The Thorsons website address is: www.thorsons.com

and *Thorsons* are trademarks of HarperCollins*Publishers* Limited.

Published by Thorsons 2001

10 9 8 7 6 5 4 3 2 1

© Michael Geary 2001

Michael Geary asserts the moral right to
be identified as the author of this work

A catalogue record for this book
is available from the British Library

ISBN 0 00 711782 5

Printed and bound in Great Britain by
Martins the Printers, Berwick upon Tweed

This humble effort is dedicated to

Sripad BV Narayana Maharaja.

He is my inspiration, teacher and friend

and has patiently revealed divine service

as the sublime goal of life.

CONTENTS

The 11 Qualities of Time

Using Time Quality to your Advantage

Experience the Quality of Time

Fundamentals

What to Expect

ACKNOWLEDGEMENTS

This book and the **panchang.com** project is the work of many people. It has been a team effort from the beginning, a team so large that it is not possible to thank everyone here by name. To all of you who have contributed, many thanks. It couldn't have been done without you.

A few people deserve special mention, not least of whom is Belinda Budge, the Publishing Director of Thorsons, who quickly grasped the ideas behind Panchang, offered her continued support and gave me the right amount of push to help me complete the manuscript on time. Her creativity, insight and guiding hand were invaluable. Many thanks to Eileen Campbell for making the introduction. Carolyn Burdet acted as editor, sounding board and steady hand in making the book what it is. Simon Haas worked long hard days doing research and helped me craft the early stages of the book.

Iain MacPhail has offered sage advice on many issues and his friendship and support are much appreciated. Thanks for hanging in there, Iain. David Embleton, Mark Farmer and Richard Prout, along with the gentlemen at Fenner's Investment Club, made Panchang possible. Their continued support and advice help steer the project through various challenges along the way.

Thanks also to Joe Mills for her hard work, sacrifice and team building; Lucie Touhy for her dedication and effort; Katherine Byles for bringing Panchang into the public eye; Crispian Mills for his friendship and belief in the project; and Trevor Anderson for looking after all the boring little details. Marcel Landman has contributed many things in the last few years – knowledge and ideas for this book, maths and coding for the **panchang.com** systems, hard work, enthusiasm and friendship. Thank you, Marcel. Henry Groover was the technical brains behind the software and website. He worked tirelessly and patiently to help craft what hadn't been done before – and with so little sleep! It hasn't always been easy, Henry, but it's been an adventure. Thank you.

Finally, and most importantly, come my family – my wife and partner Pandita, my daughters Rasa, Sudevi and Larli. They have had to tolerate a lot, make numerous sacrifices and support me in many ways for many years. This book is the fruit of their effort as much as mine. Thanks for keeping me on course.

I hope and trust that all of you are pleased by these simple efforts to share the benefits of this ancient knowledge with others.

INTRODUCTION

What, then, is time? If no one asks me,
I know; if I wish to explain to him who
asks, I know not... My soul yearns to
know this most entangled enigma.

St Augustine, *Confessions*

What would you give to have more time? Or to make more of the time you have? Most of us feel the pinch of time. It's characteristic of 21st-century life to be under pressure to do more in less time, which results in the feeling that we need more time just to keep up. 'I need 48 hours in a day' is a common cry. Work pressures, overtime, travel time, family responsibilities, conflicting agendas – these and many more factors contribute to what we now call 'time famine', the sense that we are starved of time.

This is not surprising when you consider that the average British or American professional works a 60-hour week and more, an overall increase in working time of 15 per cent in the last 20 years. Leisure time in real terms has dropped by 33 per cent. The average working person spends less than two minutes per day in meaningful conversation with their spouse and children only get 30 seconds a day. Perhaps unsurprisingly, 95 per cent of divorces are caused by a 'lack of communication'. These and many other examples point to time becoming so scarce that it is almost a kind of currency. We now tend to value people by how much time we feel we can afford to spend with them.

Meanwhile in terms of work, career and finance there are mounting pressures on companies to produce short-term profits. The strength of economies and the value of companies are measured in smaller and smaller periods of time, creating among other things the day trader. Symptomatic of short-term orientation, these buy and sell stocks in micro-periods of time. 'Going long' now means staying in the market for a month or two. This short-term economic view of life trickles down to every other aspect of life and increasingly puts people under pressure to make their time count.

All of this has spawned a number of quick-fix answers as to how we can manage our dearth of time. Some of these are as comic as suggesting that you do more things at once, for instance making mental lists while taking a shower (forget relaxing for a while under some hot water). At the other end of the spectrum others offer real value by suggesting that the secret of good time management is to do the things that really count and that are based on strong personal principles.

Regardless of the system that we use, however, the pressure continues to mount. And there are no lending institutions stepping forward to help finance our recovery from time debt. So we have time cramming, where we do more in a minute than we normally would, time slicing, where time is divided into smaller and smaller units (all of which get filled with things to do), and time leveraging, where, thanks to technology, we actually do more things concurrently – phone calls, e-mails, meetings, eating, sleeping, thinking ...

Speed is the easy answer, but hastening the pace creates even more problems, bringing a sense of urgency and eliminating the chance for those strategic moments when we should be catching our breath and considering whether the destination that we are rushing off to is the place we really want to be.

Seeing time quantitatively, as a unit to slice, allocate, reschedule and spend, is clearly not giving us the results we need. And the techno-logical promise of getting things done more quickly so that we can have a better quality of life is not being fulfilled. We have the speed and efficiency, but not the quality of life. Our momentum creates the tendency to place more tasks into the free space the speed created.

All the while this is happening we tend to lose sight of what's going on around us. The sense of moving forward, of advancing, especially as a society, blurs the details that tell us something is really wrong here. It blinds us to the longer term consequences of our actions. Need more speed? Then build faster cars – but they need more fuel, pollute the air and cause more asthma in our children and old people. The annals of environmentalists are filled with the unforeseen conse-quences of our badly thought out plans to go faster.

A fresh approach is needed at both a global and an individual level. Time is a fundamental resource and our understanding of it touches every area of life and environment. In the chain of cause and effect, time may seem remote, but in fact our use of it is a primary factor in creating the results of our actions. Time is the basic energy of our lives. How is it that it has become the enemy – the invisible force we work against?

13

To free ourselves from a slavery to time, we need to see it differently. **Panchang Moon Astrology** is a guidebook to a new understanding of time, one that is ancient but modern. It offers a new approach to time that helps us get more out of it – not by trying to put more into it, but by trying to get more from what is already there. **Panchang** means 'value for time'. We will look at time in a way that reveals its value – in ways we tend to overlook. We will see time not as an abstraction or a measurement, but as a resource that has qualities of its own – qualities that, if we are aware of them, reveal a hidden treasure in time, a treasure that can empower our actions and lives in a magical and personal way.

This is a guidebook to an adventure, a call to explore time in a way we may not have previously thought possible. As with any adventure, taking this journey means having an open mind. As Gertrude Stein said, it's a good idea to keep a little door open in the back of your head for new ideas. The ideas that we present in this book both challenge our view of time and reaffirm our intuitions of time, those feelings that are natural and often unspoken.

The focus of **Panchang Moon Astrology** is practical. It is not about dry theory or finding quick fixes to problems of contemporary 'time famine'. It's not a self-help book that does the thinking for you, but one which gets you thinking in new ways and then experimenting for yourself in order to enhance your life.

Panchang:
An Ancient Art for Modern Times

Astrology is assured recognition from
psychology, without further restriction,
because astrology represents the
summation of all psychological knowledge
of antiquity.   Carl Jung

Panchang is the practical application of Vedic astrology, an art belonging to the sages of India. It is a holistic system whose roots lie in the ancient Vedas which pre-date the Judeo-Christian era and whose Sanskrit language is considered the basis of Indo-European languages. The original texts of Vedic astrology were written by sages like Sri Parashara Muni, Sri Brighu Muni and Sri Garga Acharya. According to the Vedic tradition, these sages were divine personalities who were enlightened beings. They revealed their knowledge for the benefit of mankind, a knowledge that can help people see themselves, others and the world more clearly and deeply. In Sanskrit the art of Vedic astrology is called **Jyotish**, or 'Light', suggesting that it is a system that helps us see and that is based on the light of the planets and stars.

The Vedas are a vast body of knowledge that sets out a supportive framework for the evolution of integrated individuals and thus integrated society. Its ultimate aim is self-realization through gradual stages of material and spiritual development.

The fulfilment of people's needs is a fundamental precept to the Vedic knowledge system and so the Vedas are concerned with material well-being as well as spiritual enlightenment. As such they offer a practical and down-to-earth application of philosophical concepts. It does no good to talk about spirit when a man is hungry.

Panchang is the part of Vedic astrology whose principal aim is the creation of well-being through harmonious action with time and therefore the greater environment.

The foundation of Vedic astrology is the **sutras**, or codes, written by sages like Parashara and Brighu. These codes set out the guidelines for understanding the system and they form a kind of symbolic astrological language that allows Vedic astrologers to achieve consistent and reliable results. The dating of these works and the Vedas has been much debated, but they are anything between 2,500 and 5,000 years old. Subsequent generations of astrologers, particularly in medieval times, have commentated and expanded on the original works.

In contrast with Solar-centric Western astrology, Vedic astrology places the Moon at the centre of a person's character, life and destiny.

The Vedic sages considered time to be divine. To them the cosmos was one aspect of the Godhead, representing God in a material manifestation. This concept finds its way into the works on Vedic astrology as the **Kala-purusha** or 'divine body of time'. This is part of the Panchang-Vedic iconography which tells the story of the divine nature of time. The **Kala-purusha** (see illustration, right) shows the zodiac constellations and planets as part of a huge cosmic body and emphasizes their role as symbols or archetypes that tell the story of time. In this way they form a language that symbolizes divinity working through the mundane, for time is itself a divine energy.

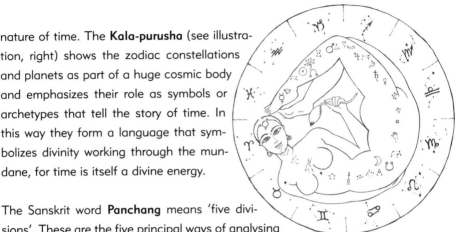

The Sanskrit word **Panchang** means 'five divisions'. These are the five principal ways of analysing time using the codes of Vedic astrology. Panchang astrology is the application of Vedic astrology in selecting times that will create material and spiritual harmony, prosperity, growth and well-being – in short, acting at the right time. Panchang was originally used by the sages for their meditations, offerings and congresses, where they would discuss philosophy and the general well-being of the populace. Vedic monarchs also used Panchang to guide their administration. Kings would use Panchang to select auspicious times to negotiate treaties, enact and implement legislation, arrange coronations, weddings and birth ceremonies, conceive qualified heirs, initiate military campaigns and diplomatic efforts, establish peace and donate to charity. Panchang was also used for civic interests such as starting education programmes and laying the foundations of new homes, palaces and civic buildings. It was used to conduct commercial enterprises, in banking, in grain storage, in the acquisition of land and the establishment of herds, farms and foundries.

With a little translation, Panchang can be put to good use in contemporary society, for business, industry, education, government, creativity or household and personal matters, as all stand to gain from the value in time that Panchang reveals.

Queen Elizabeth I, arguably Britain's best monarch, had a personal astrologer of Welsh origin, Dr John Dee, who calculated the most auspicious time for her coronation.

The idea that time has quality is an unfamiliar concept in the West, but on reflection it makes perfect sense. Our experience tells us that every day is different. Some days and times feel light, energetic and upbeat, while others are tense, chaotic, frustrating, even explosive. There are turbulent times and calm times. Some days start out one way and then shift to another mood entirely. Understanding how time has quality, how it affects us and how we can work with it is what Panchang astrology is all about.

To make this book useful to everyone we have crystallized the essence of Vedic astrology to make it easy to understand and easy to use. You do not need to be an astrologer or a philosopher to take something of this essence and use it in simple and immediate ways in your life. On the contrary, those who do not know much about the subject probably stand to gain the most.

You can read this book from beginning to end or just open it up at random to discover a new aspect of Panchang. But reading it from start to finish will give you a better picture of how the different parts fit together to create a logical, systematic view of time.

It may be important to mention at the outset that Panchang astrology is not a belief system but a knowledge system. The view of time that it gives can, I believe, be gained by different means, although undoubtedly those means will also have their respective cultural patinas.

It is my hope that **Panchang Moon Astrology** will stimulate discussion, debate and further exploration across a broad spectrum. I am not a scientist, but there may be some out there who will take up these ideas and look at them through the lens of their disciplines. Similarly, you are invited to view Panchang through your own knowledge lens. Regardless of what type of lens it is, you will find something in these ideas that will stimulate further inquiry. Please send your experience of using Panchang to **feedback@panchang.com**. We'd love to hear from you.

My experience of practising Panchang astrology over the last 20 years has been that it is not only accurate, but also offers many benefits both obvious and subtle. It is my hope that this book goes some way to make these benefits accessible to everyone.

exploring your use of time

BUSY,
BUSY
AND MORE BUSY...

There cannot be a crisis next week.
My schedule is already full.   Henry Kissinger

We are all very busy. It is the nature of contemporary life to be constantly pressed for time. We have more to do and less time to do it in. We constantly complain that we have 'no time'. We are rushing to keep up with the pace and the competition.

We measure our advancement in units, in stages, in jobs done. We aim for the completion of tasks and the production of things, which is not surprising in a consumer-based culture. The trend is away from **being** to **doing** and **having**. Even our children are measured by the speed of their progress rather than the depth and breadth of their understanding. Our addiction to speed and convenience has created a situation in which scarcity of time is on the verge of replacing the scarcity of capital.

Each of us responds to lack of time in our own way. Time management systems help us to prioritize our workload. The best of them help us focus on what is really important to us. This keeps us working on the things that matter and prevents us from losing time and energy to an increasing amount of distractions. Such systems serve as reminders that to have a good life we need to keep the important things at the centre of it. Some of us are better at this than others, but regardless of how well you are doing, the force of our culture keeps us constantly working against a tide of 'no time'.

There is more to life than increasing its speed.
Mahatma Gandhi

The no-time orientation puts pressure on us to fit as many valuable tasks into a day as we can, as though 'more' means 'better' – which it does if we are just trying to keep up. So our tendency is to find ways to pack as much as we can into our time. In New York and London, double-deal lunches have become the latest fad – swapping tables and client meetings after each course. In California, Hollywood exec-utives are teaching themselves to dream-solve problems in their sleep so that no hour, minute or second of the day is wasted.

One of the symptoms of an approaching nervous breakdown is the belief that one's work is terribly important.

Bertrand Russell

While ambition has created a few individuals who have adapted to this approach to time and who are willing to pay the price it demands, for most of us it is unnatural, unsustainable and unhealthy. For a better quality of life we need to take a step back and look at time in a new way, one that brings us into a more natural relationship with it. We need a way to work with time, not against it. We need a **with-time** approach rather than **no-time** dependencies.

Cultural conditioning tends to tell us that we don't have time to think about time, otherwise we'll fall behind. But ironically, the rush to do more using computer technology has itself contributed to a new notion of organic time. Multi-tasking, telecommuting, 'flexecutive' living and the advent of a world wide web that never sleeps have opened our minds to seeing time as concurrent, multi-directional and fluid, rather than linear and segmented. This view suggests that the real nature of time is not linear, but 'streamed', and with an acceptance of virtual time there even comes a glimpse of a multi-dimensional time.

On a personal level we all feel the need to connect to a view of time that is more natural and more meaningful to us. Panchang offers us a view of time which allows us to use the quantity without losing the quality. It all comes not so much from **doing** things differently as from **seeing** things differently.

Think about it

Free yourself from being pressured by a shortage of time. Rather than cramming more in, make space for a new approach – keep an open mind to new ways of seeing time.

Give it a try

《 Take stock of the time in your life. How would you describe your approach to it? Do you see time as a friend, enemy, resource, life energy, experience...?

《 How do you value your time? How much free time did you have yesterday to think about the really important matters of your life? Take a little time each day to reflect on the *really* important issues, those that are often neglected or forgotten in the rush of the day.

LIVE IT
INSTEAD OF
COUNTING IT

Not everything that counts can be counted, and not everything that can be counted counts. Einstein

The dreary bits of life are often the things that must be done because they must be done. It is not always easy or even possible to change this, which is why they can seem dreary.

The majority of us have at one time or another been in a job or situation that didn't suit us, but we were there because we had to be there. Your job was probably different from my job (toll-booth attendant), but one thing we probably shared was clock watching. With every glance at the clock the minutes dilated to become much more than 60 ticks of the second hand. Funny how those ticks were very different when I was with Wendy, my girlfriend. I don't know what you did to find relief from minutes that passed as hours, but luckily I found that I could read bits of poetry in between the arrival of cars. I chose to live the moments rather than count them. In doing so I filled them with more than just distraction, I filled them with value that changed my experience of a minute sometimes to the same quality of experience, or better, than when I was with Wendy (sorry, Wendy). Rilke's **Duino Elegies** took a minute and brought a night of angel-filled reveries that expanded to something close to timelessness. Sometimes I was still in that state while I was punching tickets and collecting dollar bills. I had to do the dreary job, but I chose to be alive in doing it, to bring something of myself to it. I chose to live it as best I could. If your work is dreary and the time drags, why not bring something of yourself into your time? The experience will improve both for you and the people you interact with.

"If you knew time as well as I do," said the Hatter, "you wouldn't talk about wasting it."

Lewis Carroll, *Alice's Adventures in Wonderland*

In counting time we tend to lose the magic of it. As a measurement it becomes meaningless. It is as **experience** that time has value and purpose. It may be stating the obvious, but if we look around us, we find that the rush from A to B lessens the experience and its value. Time becomes something we consume, a moment or an hour, but really it is the treasure of our life. In consuming time **we** become the commodity, not time itself. Do we really want to 'kill time' like this?

To make time magical again, we have to see it as a child sees it, not in the way we have been taught or conditioned, but through the eyes of discovery. When you walk to the shops with a young child, the event becomes a journey of discovery, not a goal to reach. If the person accompanying this young child on their voyage of discovery happens to be 70 years old, they may be counting time too, but the chances are they'll be counting each valuable moment in their life, sipping every experience from the elixir of life. Whatever our age, we need to connect with the timelessness of childhood or old age to discover the value of the moment.

Time becomes something meaningful when we are in it. Then it becomes ours and then it counts. Does an athlete measure success as the time it takes to run the 100m sprint? The coach does the counting, while the athlete is living the magic of the moment. They are not thinking of time, but are focused on form, breathing, consciousness and attitude, clarity and goal. Gold comes when all these harmoniously combine – and then the athlete looks at the clock.

When you have put your all into something, your total being, time actually becomes timeless. It is then that we feel something close to eternity.

One realizes the full importance of time only when there is little of it left. Every man's greatest capital asset is his unexpired years of productive life.

P.W. Litchfield

Think about it

Think about how time is a living experience rather than a way to measure the duration of an experience. How does the quality of an experience alter your perception of time? Expand your time and your experience of time by becoming aware of how time is your own personal experience of life.

Give it a try

❨ Think about a joyous experience. Were you conscious of time? Did time have any meaning to you in terms of the experience? Do you know how long it lasted? Could you compare the value of the experience with the quantity of time it took to have it? What is more important – having the experience or counting its duration?

Time can be contracted or dilated. In the time span of a film you can cover seven generations of love, pain, loss and gain or just experience the events in one afternoon of love. Think about how this relativity of time works in your own life.

look
around
you

BEGIN PAYING ATTENTION TO THE QUALITY OF TIME

The most important thing in communication is to hear what isn't being said.   Peter F. Drucker

There is a quality to every moment. While I may not share your feelings about the weather, we both share the weather itself if we are in the same place. The same is true of time.

While some of us are more sensitive to our surroundings than others, we can all have a sense of time quality and the subtle influences around us. If we open our eyes to this, time becomes quite magical. We can feel what the day will be like – even before it happens. For some people this is a radical idea, for others quite natural. But if we begin paying attention to the quality of time, we will all begin to see its effects in the world around us.

Almost everyone has had a sense of what a day will bring before it arrives. On waking in the morning a little voice says, 'It's going to be a good day today...' or you step outside the door and realize that the day is going to be 'hard work'. This quiet whisper of awareness comes in unexpected ways, appearing as events, conditions, moods and exchanges that you encounter during your day. Acknowledge the hints and you will gradually become attuned to levels of awareness that you previously thought impossible.

In general women tend to be more open to their intuition, whereas men generally tend to disregard inner whispers or external clues as 'irrational' or 'emotional'. Men like to explain something, make sense of it, make it logical and put it into a spreadsheet. But as even scientists have to admit sometimes, life doesn't always fit into explainable blocks.

Listening to those whispers of awareness means hearing what is coming to us unconsciously. Our unconscious is more honest than we are, braver, more direct. But it speaks in the language of dreams to give us the chance to take it or leave it. In the same way we can take or leave the subtle messages of life, time and the world around us, but if we leave them, we don't see the whole picture. This may be momentarily more comfortable, but if we are stubborn and ignore the message then life tends to become tougher, to rock us out of our slumber. Dreams become nightmares and life's neat and tidy parcels begin to fall apart. Listening to the whisper is a lot easier in the long run.

In becoming aware of time's quality, we start listening to the environment. What is the common thread running through the day? It is normal to be aware of it, but usually we don't attribute it to an intrinsic quality of time, but to chance. However, the sages of most cultures tell us that chance is simply nature talking and the Vedas say there is no chance, it only appears that way due to a poor field of vision.

Paying attention to our environment means being conscious of the magic of synchronicity. It also means being aware of what nature is telling us about whether it's time to act or to wait. Is it a good time to ask your boss for a rise, ask someone out on a date or ask your partner for some help? What is happening in your environment is reflecting the quality of time. It is telling you when you should go with the flow and avoid imposing your will and when you should move forward with confidence. Listening to this alone, if nothing else, will make you more skilled in dealing with people.

Think about it

Open up to the greater natural environment. Explore how you are part of a natural pattern of events, one that has your unique stamp on it but is also larger than you personally. You are a participant in a greater natural theatre called life.

Give it a try

☾ Look around you. Make a mental note of how people seem to be feeling or reacting to the day's events. Do you notice a pattern?

☾ How do you feel today? What's the mood? Is this a tough, energetic, pleasant or aggressive day?

BE OPEN
TO THE MOMENTS
THAT DO COUNT

I'd rather have a moment of wonderful than a
lifetime of nothing special.

From the movie *Steel Magnolias*

Important thoughts are timeless. They come in a moment and often
when we least expect them. Making the most of our time means being
receptive to them when they come. They may come disguised as con-
versations, inspiration, dreams, sudden breakthroughs. To honour
them and do them justice we need to listen to them, because they are
often disguised or quiet. If we use only 10 per cent of our brain, then
maybe it is just a matter of listening a little more to what the other 90
per cent is saying.

The greatest inventions and discoveries were made by people who
took an intuitive approach, rather than a rigid approach, to time.
These people often worked into the night, or at the oddest hours.
Some of the best ideas come at the strangest times, maybe in the
night or just before going to bed or waking up, completely disregarding
formal schedules and timetables.

One moment of insight can be worth a lifetime's effort. But we need to recognize it and to take the time to listen to it. Too busy can mean too deaf. To hear what is being said can take some practice.

So let yourself daydream from time to time. Daydreaming can be very productive. It can keep us fresh, replenish creativity, help us cope with the pace of our world. The times when we shut out the chatter of the world around us, pull our senses in for a bit and connect with our inner self can be the most productive part of our day. Daydreaming, meditating, listening, whatever you want to call it, creates opportunity in a way that makes the busyness of doing appear meagre indeed.

To see a World in a Grain of Sand,

And a Heaven in a Wild Flower,

Hold Infinity in the palm of your hand,

And Eternity in an hour.

William Blake, *Auguries of Innocence*

Think about it

Take a new approach to time, one in which you take time to make time. Be open to the quiet inner moments which bring deep value. These moments come naturally and effortlessly. Be ready to receive them as gifts when they announce their arrival.

Give it a try

(Recollect an important moment, one that brought revelation and understanding. How much time did it take? Where did it take place?

(Take time to make time. Create a sacred time in your day. Early morning may be best.

During this time allow yourself simply to be. Be with yourself and listen to what comes. It may come as thought, words, colours, feelings or pictures, according to your nature.

Make a note of whatever comes to you and as you progress in your understanding of Panchang these impressions will string together to create a big picture of what is happening with your time and in your life.

This will help you develop intuition and feeling, which is very important in being effective, creative and getting more from your time.

(Panchang helps you plan for good moments in advance. If you know when magic moments are likely to happen, you can make space for them to happen.

Be free to daydream from time to time. It may seem impractical or a waste of time, but in fact it may be more productive than your harder-working moments. The Japanese understand this. If someone is daydreaming or looking out the window they do not interrupt them, whereas they feel free to interrupt someone who is working at their desk.

time

cycles

THINK OF TIME AS CYCLICAL, NOT LINEAR

Our life is an apprenticeship to the truth that around every circle another can be drawn; that there is no end in nature, but every end is a beginning, and under every deep a lower deep opens.

Ralph Waldo Emerson

Everything in nature is cyclical – day and night, the seasons, the phases of the Moon, the ebb and flow of tides, fertility cycles, birth and death – everything is repeated again and again. Weather patterns, blossoms, harvests come again and again. Human events also occur cyclically. Throughout history, social, economic and political themes have repeated themselves over and over – boom and bust, repression and liberation, conservative and liberal social trends, the natural cycles of expansion and recession... All these have their part to play in human affairs. The details may change, but the themes are familiar, the patterns recognizable and the lessons we can learn from them constant.

The cycles of time are at the core of Panchang astrology, which sees time as a dynamic, even spiritual energy that energizes the workings of nature. For many reasons the common view of time is linear – the beginning-and-end model. It is easy to see why we think like this, especially in a consumerist culture of make, use, throw away. However, we are beginning to see the long-term effects of our use-it, consume-it view. To some extent we placate our nagging conscience with recycling, while failing to address the deeper issues – that our failing resources are the result of a linear view of nature, one that doesn't require the replenishment and rejuvenation of cycles. If we look closely at nature there is a perpetual conservation of energy at work, a recycling of energies and resources in all things. A fundamental principle of physics points to the dynamic behind all this: matter and energy are interchangeable and cannot be destroyed.

There are other reasons why we tend to view things using the beginning-and-end model. We see it all around us as the birth and death principle, which has been incorporated into a few religious and philosophical models, arguably with dire results in terms of our overall world view. Nevertheless many of the world's philosophies and religions see birth and death as cyclical. People don't die, their bodies die. Their energy goes on to reincarnate somewhere else. Hinduism, Buddhism, the mystical traditions of Judaism, Islam, even early Christianity saw death as the changing of bodies, not the final end of a soul's journey. The Vedas describe this as **samsara**, or the great wheel of birth and death, which represented **moksha**, or the soul's gradual journey towards enlightenment and liberation from the limits of matter.

So, whether you look at the cyclical aspect of nature and time in a philosophical way or simply take what you see in nature, from small seashells to great swirling galaxies, the pattern of cycles, circles and repetition is axiomatic.

It is important to emphasize Panchang's cyclical view as it lies at the core of its ability to predict the patterns of time energy in the future and to analyse their influence in the past. As an astrological system, Panchang uses the planets and constellations to make its calculations and analysis. Planetary movements, especially those of the Moon, are cyclical and reliable and offer a way of knowing the quality of future time.

Why Does Time Appear to Move in a Straight Line?

Most people think of time as a linear, rather than cyclical. This is because our experience of time is generally microcosmic. We see it very close up. And if you take a minute segment of a circle at great magnification, it appears as a straight line. The ocean horizon appears as fairly flat when standing on the beach, but from the space shuttle it is definitely round.

Standing back from events in time we begin to see cyclical patterns emerge. Time appears as waves of fluctuating quality, events that rise and fall and can be plotted on graphs that represent conditions in the economy, the weather, the tides, the seasons or our own lives.

So time can be seen as line, wave and circle. Viewed up close, like the ocean horizon it appears as a line. From another angle it is a circle, with qualities, conditions and events returning again and again. And from yet a more distant perspective there is a progressive nature to time. Our understanding of time is based on how we view it – up close, from further away or from very far away. A view of time is like a view of a fractal – you can see it as a line, a circle, or a line made up of circles, or a circle made up of lines made up of circles ... endlessly.

To come full circle in time doesn't mean going back to the same point in calendar time. We won't have to witness the events of the 1970s or 1980s again, but we will at some point return to the same themes, challenges or issues that previous generations faced. In our brave new world the possibilities of genetic research, for example, are unique. No other generation has faced the details of this particular challenge, yet previous generations did face equally difficult moral and ethical dilemmas – equal at least in terms of their own social and cultural circumstances.

Cycles come again and again, but they move along a progressive line – time's arrow. We can see this in our own lives, where seasons are repeated, lessons recur until we learn them, themes disappear and reappear over and over, and with each occurrence we have moved along time's arrow.

Ancient traditions and Vedic sages did not see time as an arrow travelling inexorably in a straight line, but as a pattern of cycles that had certain qualities that were repeated in theme and general influence. The linear concept of time emerged later in ancient Greek philosophy and was adopted by Christianity in AD 300–400.

Again, Again and Again

The Vedic idea of time is one where time cycles are repeated because universes are repeated – they are created, destroyed and created again and again, very much like bodies. Vedic time cycles describe periods that range from staggering in scope – cosmically massive **Manvantaras**, which are 90,720,000,000 Solar years – down to atomic seconds – calculated as the amount of time it takes to travel past a **paramanu**, or particle of sunlight – with the projected lifespan of the universe being approximately 388,000 billion of our Solar years.

This lifespan is made up of **yugas** or aeons, four of which add up to 6,480,000 Solar years and the smallest of which is our current **Kali Yuga**, which lasts for 432,000 years, approximately 5,000 of which have already passed.

Each of the four main **yugas** has a unique nature and quality of time, represented by gold (**Sattya Yuga**), silver (**Tretta Yuga**), copper (**Dvarpara Yuga**) and iron (**Kali Yuga**). The qualities of each successive **yuga** are considered progressively degenerative from the first to the last, after which a new cycle begins. Each **yuga** may be likened to a kind of cosmic season, with **Sattya** being the spring and **Kali** being the winter. These macro-cycles of time quality and their influence are represented in successively smaller cycles and sub-cycles, and touch all things in nature.

All living entities have similar cycles of time quality that influence their lives. Each of us has a cyclical influence of the macro-environment that affects us and a micro or personal set of time cycles that account for our personal circumstances and the themes of our life experience.

Panchang astrology takes into account the nature of both the general time cycles and the personal time cycles, then analyses them and compares their interaction and compatibility to draw conclusions about the quality of time for any person, business, government or organization.

The cycles of time and their qualities are the principal subject of Panchang astrology. Understanding their nature, influence and energy helps us determine the quality of time for anyone at any place.

Everything the power of the world does is done in a circle.

The sky is round and I have heard that the Earth is round like a ball and so are all the stars. The wind, in its greatest power, whirls.

Birds make their nests in circles, for theirs is the same religion as ours.

The sun comes forth and goes down again in a circle. The moon does the same and both are round. Even the seasons form a great circle in their changing and always come back again to where they were.

The life of a man is a circle from childhood to childhood, and so it is in everything where power moves. Our tepees were round like the nests of birds, and these were always set in a circle, the nation's hoop, a nest of many nests, where the Great Spirit meant for us to hatch our children.

Black Elk, Oglala Sioux

ORGANIZING
YOUR TIME

To get all there is out of living, we must employ our time wisely, never being in too much of a hurry to stop and sip life, but never losing our sense of the enormous value of a minute.   Robert Updegraff

Sociological studies have shown two major character inclinations when it comes to approaching and organizing our time. One is highly structured 'monochronic' or 'M-time', the other highly intuitive and fluid 'polychronic' or 'P-time'. In practice it is a rare occurrence for anyone to incline towards just one type of time. Usually we combine both but have a strong tendency toward one or the other. One is not necessarily better than the other; in fact both can work in harmony and both have their place in an effective relationship with time.

Two Types of Thinking – A Comparison

Monochronic M-time Attitudes towards Time

Do one thing at a time.

Schedule co-ordinates activity – appointment time is rigid.

Time is inflexible.

Time is money.

Work time is clearly separated from personal time.

Polychronic P-time Attitudes towards Time

Do several things at a time.

Relationships co-ordinate activity – appointment time is flexible.

Time is flexible; time is fluid.

The time is right – now. Let's go.

Business is a form of socializing.

Other M-time Attitudes

Task-oriented; the goal is task achievement.

Accustomed to short-term relationships.

Other P-time Attitudes

People oriented; the goal is working on relationships with people.

Strong tendency to build lifetime relationships.

Seldom borrows or lends.	Borrows and lends things often and easily.
Adheres rigidly to plans.	Changes plans often and easily.

Examples of **M-time** Countries

Examples of **P-time** Countries

USA	France, Spain, Greece and Italy
Germany	India
Japan	Australia
England	The Caribbean, African countries

DO YOU TEND TOWARDS M-TIME OR P-TIME?

Deadlines are the milestones you pass on your way to completion. Peter Gabriel to Crispian Mills

M-time

Monochronic time (M-time) is oriented towards tasks, schedules and procedures. M-time is tangible; we speak of time being saved, spent, wasted, lost or made up, crawling, killed and running out. M-time is a commodity that is valued in units and measures.

In an M-type culture, people work in a linear and orderly way, intent on getting one job completed before starting the next. M-type thinking is 'one at a time' thinking. A good example of this is the queues that form in shops because sales assistants deal with customers one at a time. People take a ticket at the delicatessen counter and wait to be served. The British and the Americans are accustomed to this way of doing things. In this model of thinking, waiting patiently is a virtue.

There is often a monetary value attributed to time in M-type environments. In a sense time has a production-line function, it is something that happens as a means to a desired end.

Task achievement is the goal for M-type people. Goals and deliverables are their **raison d'être**. Having the flexibility to respond to changing conditions is difficult for M-types. Sometimes changeability is even seen as a weakness. The emphasis is on logic, analysis, measurement and vision. The end-game is the main focus, not the path or the experience of getting there.

P-time

We live in a monochronic society that is time driven, clock obsessed and insists on seeing tasks completed in a linear, orderly and logical fashion, but for thousands of years our brains have worked in a polychronic way. That means being willing to change plans and deal with many things happening at the same time, without becoming frustrated by our inability to hit deadlines one by one. Ancient cultures were predominantly P-type, especially as they tended to be closer in their thinking and daily activity to the conditions of nature and the changing seasons. Mediterranean cultures are the best example in the modern world of P-type dominant culture in action.

Polychronic or P-time places our relationships with people at the centre of our activities. Agendas are flexible and there to facilitate the chance for personal exchange, not to rigidly mark blocks of time. Schedules are flexible and readily changed to accommodate the needs of people. Meetings are a 'meeting of minds' – they begin and end whenever the participants feel the time is right. Punctuality – nearly sacred to an M-type – is not so important for a P-type. They understand that the changeable nature of time means things pop up that need attention, so there is no point getting worked up about people being late.

Anthropologist Edward T. Hall describes P-time in this way:

P-time stresses involvement of people and completion of transactions rather than adherence to pre-set schedules ...

For polychronic people, time is seldom experienced as 'wasted,' and is apt to be considered a point rather than a ribbon or a road, but that point is often sacred ...

Polychronic cultures are by their very nature oriented to people.

Any human being who is naturally drawn to other human beings and who lives in a world dominated by human relationships will be either pushed or pulled toward the polychronic end of the time spectrum.

If you value people, you must hear them out and cannot cut them off simply because of a schedule.[1]

P-type cultures have a natural tendency to multi-tasking. People do many things at once and deal with many people at once, even though this approach tends to punctuate exchanges with the necessary attention that is given to someone arriving in a conversation or space. P-type people consider people more important than tasks and are insulted if they are neglected in favour of a task or process. P-type thinking is more community-oriented. It places a high value on personal exchange, even if this is only pleasantries. P-types would never think of life's little courtesies as a 'waste of time'.

If you approach time polychronically you will work happily on many tasks at once. You won't think twice about changing your plans at a moment's notice. Furthermore you won't get too worried or stressed over deadlines. Deadlines are points that mark the beginning and end of cycles, and cycles are events that transpire **naturally**. They are a part of nature over which we have no control – or can agree not to control. To a predominantly polychronic person, time always has a purpose because the emphasis is on experience and exchange. Time **is** life.

M-time vs P-time

When these two different ways of looking at time come together at work or in a social setting, misunderstandings can arise. People with a monochronic attitude may feel as if nothing is being accomplished and become impatient with the open-ended polychronic sense of timing. To P-type people timescales depend on individual talents, but they will be expressed in relation to whatever crises or celebrations are going on in their personal lives.

Later we will show how M-time and P-time can be harmonized with Panchang.

Think about it

Think about how you approach time. Which of the two ways of working describes you? Or are you a combination of the two?

Give it a try

☾ If you approach time more in one way than the other, can you borrow something from the other? Can you use it to inspire a new personal approach to time?

☾ Can you imagine a combination of M-time and P-time that would result in a highly effective, integrated character?

1 Edward T. Hall, *The Dance of Life: The Other Dimension of Time,* Anchor Press/Doubleday, 1983, pp. 43–50

53

SUN AND MOON, A PRODUCTIVE COMBINATION

The intuitive mind is a sacred gift and the rational mind is a faithful servant. We have created a society that honours the servant and has forgotten the gift.

Einstein

Panchang is a specialized application of Vedic astrology and uses the symbolism of the planets, including the Sun and the Moon. Both are important, but there is a special emphasis on the Moon, as it symbolizes the areas of our life that are closest to us – mind and learning, the emotions, heart, goodwill, mother and home, grace and intellect, to name just a few.

The Sun and Moon and their harmonious relationship symbolize the integrated self, the whole person and a happy life. The Sun and Moon represent the masculine and feminine principles respectively, the principle of opposites, the dualities in nature symbolized by the yin–yang symbol of Buddhism. If they are in harmony in a chart, integration and balance follow, whereas discord in their relationship represents a struggle or striving. Their interaction in a chart therefore symbolically represents the possibility of harmony and disharmony and the many shades of variety in between. Panchang incorporates both principles in its approach to time – M-time and P-time are symbolized by the Sun and Moon respectively. Neither is more important than the other. Ideally, they work together to create balanced life and time.

Understanding this symbolism helps us understand the language of time quality, which offers us a map of the energies and influences of time and a better way of using the dynamics of time effectively.

M-time is Solar

Masculine, linear, focused, directed, forceful

Astrologically speaking, M-time and the Sun are synonymous. Both are driven, energetic, logical, structured, disciplined, wilful, determined and goal-oriented. The emphasis is on process and formula.

The Sun represents authority, leadership, law, accountability and management. All tend to have a strong M-time orientation. The regal nature of the Sun is symbolized as the King, with Leo its sign – the order, dignity, protocol and diplomacy of court are Solar in nature. These qualities are all M-time, especially regarding interpersonal dealings, where diplomacy sets the tone for what can and cannot be said.

When you think of M-time, think of the Sun and its meaning. This will help you understand the mechanics of M-time and the right way to use it.

Authority is a good example of this. To live under a benevolent leader, manager or political structure is desirable. In these cases authority is tempered with understanding, listening, generosity, empathy and support. Discipline and rules are there to give support to the finer sides of our nature. Conversely a bureaucracy that has lost its connection to the needs of the people it serves is harsh, inflexible and a pain to deal with. 'The rules are the rules' – never mind why they were created in the first place.

The Solar nature of M-time can be expressed in almost any area of life. Considering the positive and negative aspects of it will enable us to see how it works in daily life.

Sun's Radiance: Positive Qualities

Purpose; mission; energy; action; authority; protectiveness; dignity; direction; hierarchy; life purpose; ambition; strength of will; stability; reliability; foundation.

Sun's Shadow: Negative Qualities

Domination; alienation; imposition of will; aggression; ego-centricity; superiority complex; acquisitive; insensitive; lacking empathy; force of influence based on insecurity.

P-time is Lunar

Feminine, flexible, creative, flowing, adaptable

P-time's astrological nature is Lunar. Both P-time and Lunar qualities are soft, feminine, gentle, empathetic, emotive, giving, creative, intuitive, inspired, nurturing, thoughtful and organic. The emphasis is on **being**.

The Moon represents the mother, mother's milk, tenderness, support, guidance through nurturing, sacrifice (not in a biblical sense but in giving for another's benefit), home, hearth and kitchen, the heart, mind, emotions, digestion, sanctuary and retreat. All of these are oriented towards experience and the art of living. The regal nature of the Moon is symbolized by the Queen or the Earth Mother, and its sign is Cancer, which tempers the will and authority of the masculine energy represented by the Sun. The Queen is the cosmic character who is courteous and flexible in court dealings and gets things done not so much through pomp but through discretion, secret liaisons and talks, alliances, clever dealings and loyalty created by looking after those who serve her – in other words, all those people-oriented things which would never be served by the strictness of protocol. All of this symbolizes P-time and its people-first view. And it is a pointer to how you can use P-time effectively in your life.

To live and work under the protection of a caring queen, mentor or social structure is good fortune. These all give and nurture with a view to seeing the individual grow into the best they can be. Pure giving is tempered, however, by the discipline offered by the Sun, just as a gardener may give water and fertilizer to a plant, but may also bind it to ensure it grows straight and strong.

When the archetypes of queen, mother or mentor lose their caring root, they become disruptive and disorienting, creating confusion and sowing the seeds of self-doubt, insecurity and fear. Life takes on an irrational, groundless and fickle aspect, which makes growth difficult.

Looking at the positive and negative expression of the P-time Lunar principle can help us understand the best and the worst of the P-time approach to life.

Moon's Glow: Positive Qualities

Helpful; sweet; uplifting; calming; nurturing; supportive; creative; reflective; inspired; charitable; social; meditative; constructive emotions; insight; empathy; expressive; communicative; incorporative (reduces alienation).

Moon's Shadow: Negative Qualities

Unstable; aimless; moody; irrational; negative and destructive emotions; depression; deception; illusion; lunacy; chaotic; unrealistic; delusional; intense hankering; wanton desire that is unattainable.

Think about it

Consider how landscaping and nurturing can create a beautiful garden, how mother and father can work together to raise children, how inspiration and perspiration bring a good idea into being.

Give it a try

☽ Reflect on any important accomplishment in your life. Remember when the idea first came to you. Remember the energy and the effort you spent in making it happen. Remember how your intuition guided you to achieve this result. Remember the satisfaction and fulfilment of putting your plan into action. This reflects the effective union of Solar and Lunar energy in your life.

☽ Using the same example, think about the things that went wrong. Was there too much Solar or too much Lunar energy? Was your approach too strongly M-time or too strongly P-time? Did you force something or were you too passive? What sense of balance did you learn from the experience?

The poet and novelist Robert Graves believed absolutely in the power of the moon.

He was convinced that what he called 'the white goddess' produces in us a kind of deep intuitive knowledge of the Earth and its secrets – that same knowledge that still makes 'old-fashioned' farmers plant their crops during a waxing moon and reap them during a waning moon.

Graves went on to assert that modern man has turned his back on the lunar world and prefers instead the harsh, rational light of the sun. As a result, he has lost the powers of intuition, which prefer to bask in a cooler and more mysterious light.[2]

2   Jenny Hope and James Chapman, 'Moonstruck', *Daily Mail,* 13 December 2000

PANCHANG: WHERE P-TIME AND M-TIME WORK TOGETHER

Until we manage TIME, we can manage nothing else. Peter F. Drucker

Panchang combines P-time and M-time thinking into a holistic view which draws on their respective strengths.

Panchang places P-time at the heart of its approach to time. As we have suggested, an effective use of time incorporates the creative, flexible and intuitive qualities of P-time. This is where creative and inspired energy translate into vision. P-time is a mine of opportunity. It is the driving energy for any organization.

M-time's most dynamic application is when it serves a P-time oriented core. If managed well, M-time's focus on process, deadlines, targets and structure gives P-time the foundation it needs to give form to its creativity. P-time can then realize its potential by being channelled through M-time energy and drive to accomplish tasks. Working together they are like the combination of left and right brain. As any successful artist will attest, discipline and direction are essential to making ideas a reality.

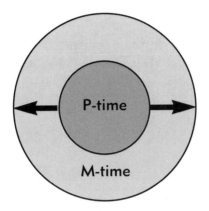

Panchang time

The Panchang view that time has quality sits at the centre of the P-time circle. Quality takes precedence over quantity. It is more important to do the right thing, if only for a short time, than to be working at the wrong thing for a long time. Panchang time quality supports the intuitive and creative, and harmonizes our actions with our environment.

Panchang's M-time aspect tells us when qualities in time exist well in advance of their arrival. It gives the structure and foundation for action, where timing is everything, and allows us to recognize patterns of qualities, influences and conditions as they arise. Panchang's M-time tells us that doing this task now is a bad idea because we will waste our time, and in M-time thinking, time is money.

In effect the M-time aspect supports P-time activity by saying 'This is a great time for creative work, team building, pure thought, etc' or 'This is a great time to do routine work because the energies of time are so unstable that it may be frustrating to attempt a creative effort where harmony and serenity are needed.'

Panchang's natural combination of both types of thinking creates mutual support for both. One isn't better than the other, except in regard to specific uses. Panchang time makes the best use of both – at any time.

Think about it

Combining the best of both P-time and M-time creates a powerful and personal use of time. Each brings the best out of the other.

Give it a try

(((Create P-time space through creativity, flexibility, daydreaming, meditation and inspiration. Support this with M-time planning. They are separate but complementary approaches. Select a creative project and structure its realization with M-time planning.

(((In the process of doing this, take time to recharge and refocus with P-time space. Make a note of your inspirations and insights. After the process of creative brainstorming, put some time into making the practical sides of the project a reality.

ten
panchang

principles

TIME HAS QUALITY

Have you ever thought about how one day is different from the next? Have you ever noticed how the mood can shift in the course of a day from fierce or frustrating to settled and stable? That is the first clue that time has its own particular quality.

We don't usually think in terms of time having an intrinsic quality. We usually think of time in abstract terms – a slot we fill with things to do or a date we cross off the calendar. The ancient Vedas, however, see time as a web that weaves through all existence, tying together space, matter, action and experience. Vedic sages would arrange the most important events in the year to coincide with auspicious times – times which gave their actions a supportive, powerful energy. To them, time was like most things we experience in nature – there were good days, bad days and lots of moments in between.

In simple terms the sages understood that some times have a constructive, helpful and loving quality, whereas others are challenging, disruptive, unstable or destructive. They would perform activities that had a nature which matched the quality of the time – using inherently stable times for building, investing and growing, energetic times for sports communication and education, and challenging or disruptive times for battle, reclamation or debate.

The knowledge of the Vedas is based on the **gunas,** or three principal qualities or modes of nature: **sattva,** stability and goodness; **rajas,** industry and passion; and **tamas,** entropy and ignorance. These three combine to create the diversity we experience in nature, just as the three primary colours (red, yellow and blue) combine to create the spectrum of visible colour.

This radical but ancient view of time helps us get more out of our time and our lives. Time becomes a more powerful tool, because we see it for the rich resource it is. Without this view we tend to either waste time quality unconsciously or use it successfully by sheer serendipity – what we usually call 'being at the right place at the right time'. But once we are aware of the quality of time it opens the door for us to explore ourselves and the world around us in a magical and revealing way.

Think about it

Think about how everything around you has quality. Why shouldn't time also have quality?

Give it a try

☾ Have an open mind and test the premise. Be mindful of your environment. Observe, reflect and note the moods and influences of each day and how they ebb and flow.

☾ Explore with friends and colleagues the idea that time has quality. Ask them if they have experienced such a thing. How do they express it?

TIME IS PERSONAL

Time is the substance from which I am made. Time is a river which carries me along, but I am the river ...

Jorge Luis Borges

Every moment in time has its own unique quality. There is a general quality that colours our environment and the field of experience in which we operate. Simultaneously we all experience the quality of any given moment. How we 'relate' to the quality of any moment depends on our nature. Some times suit us, others are jarring and some are neutral. Times that are in harmony with our nature tend to help and support us. Those times which are out of synch with our personality can create confusion or discord, while times that have a neutral aspect tend to be experienced as uneventful or routine. The most important factor is how we can use either a helpful or challenging time effectively.

Some times are difficult. We have all experienced them. There are days when everyone in the office seems on edge or grumpy. The quality of time at moments like these is most likely challenging, unstable or disruptive. Nevertheless you personally may be feeling fine. You may even enjoy the sense of things being on edge. You may feel good in the chaos and somehow be able to make it work for you. Although this particular time may be challenging for many people, it may suit your personality – maybe it complements your way of doing things, it supports and enthuses you.

Conversely it may be a sweet, tender, easy-going day. Everyone around you is on a high – which somehow only serves to make you feel grumpy and anti-social. The general quality of time may be upbeat, but you may not feel that you can use what's on offer to the fullest. And of course if you compare yourself to everyone else, you'll probably feel even worse!

These are simple but illustrative examples. The point is that different personalities respond differently to the nature of any moment of time. One day may be sweet and you can make use of it, another day may be sweet and you can make nothing of it. These moments do not occur at random – they have a complex pattern which can be charted and understood, before or after the event.

The emphasis is on our ability to use any time to our personal advantage. A high-energy, go-getting person who derives a sense of accomplishment from saying 'I've gone out there and done it' may work well with the high energy of a chaotic period of time. They can make breakthroughs and move forward on a wave of aggressive energy. A quiet, introspective person, on the other hand, may find a chaotic time too disruptive. They may find a steady, nurturing time more productive.

As we learn about the subtle aspects of time quality we can begin to use them consciously and effectively to empower our important daily actions.

Think about it

Everyone around you may be living through the same general quality of time, but each moment has a unique relationship with you. You have your own unique personal clock, seasons, cycles and eras. Panchang helps you map your journey through those life cycles.

Give it a try

☾ Think about your major life events and changes. While you experienced these upheavals, life went serenely on for other people around you. Do you remember the different phases in your life so far? Most of us can characterize them as good, bad, easy, challenging, growing, stagnant and the like. Do you remember how long they lasted? Do you recall how you felt, especially when they shifted from bad to good or good to bad?

TIME
IS LIFE

Twenty years from now you will be more
disappointed by the things that you didn't do than
by the ones you did do. So throw off the bowlines.
Sail away from the safe harbour. Catch the trade
winds in your sails. Explore. Dream. Discover.

Mark Twain

Time is the most valuable thing a man can spend.

Laertius Diogenes

Time is at once the most valuable and the most
perishable of all our possessions.

John Randolph

If you were told you had a year left to live, how would you spend that time? The chances are you would suddenly see it as precious and passing, and it would take on a personal poignancy. Every moment would count in a way it never did when it was a blank cheque. Actually your time had that value all along – because your time is your life.

It is important to be aware of mortality now and then. It helps us focus and puts things in perspective. When viewed through the lens of our mortality our sense of time distorts. The sunny summer afternoon that never ends is insignificant in time in relation to our whole lifespan. As we age our sense of time and what we want from it changes. What's important now may not seem to have any value with hindsight.

Having a sense of time as a precious resource is age-old wisdom. All the money in the world cannot buy you a lost moment of your time. So it's smart to invest your time well. Do we really want to kill time? It's a transient, tentative wealth and yet it's the basis of everything we hope to gain from life.

The Vedic view is that time is something to transcend, to rise above and go beyond – as Blake said, to experience 'Eternity in an hour'. To do this we have to use time well.

Being conscious of time and transcending it seems contradictory, but on closer examination, it makes good sense. It helps us to look at time as a finite temporal resource within which lies an eternity of experience and wealth. Regardless of our personal aim in life, time is our currency. Making more of it makes more of ourselves.

There is also a recognition that personalized time is highly effective time. Recent books, including **Faster, Blur, The Metronomic Society** and **A Geography of Time**, suggest that how we customize our time is set to become one of the biggest psychological and sociological challenges we are likely to face over the next thousand years. Panchang takes personalization of time to the next level.

According to human resource experts, a person with a monochronic approach fits in best in the modern workplace: he is time-driven, works in a linear and orderly way and is intent on getting one job completed before starting the next.

However, this is about to change.

More and more people want to be in control of their own time. 'It's going to be one of the great cultural fights over the next decade,' says (trends forecaster) Pillot de Chenecey, who has been monitoring the situation. 'We've had direct action against companies for their abuses of the environment, and their treatment of the Third World. In the future, it will be for their inability to work time to our advantage rather than theirs.'

Martin Raymond, 'The Time Machine'

QUALITY
VS QUANTITY

Remember that life is not measured in
hours but in accomplishments. James A. Pike

Most of us know that quality is more important than quantity. As Einstein
implied, one minute with Marilyn Monroe is better than one minute with
your hand on a hot-plate. Thus the quality of an experience tends to contract or dilate our experience of time's duration. We naturally place an
emphasis on quality, unless of course the two combine to create the best
of both worlds. We want both, of course, but rarely get it.

We all know that quality is important, but the modern fixation with
counting time can create problems. So much of our lives is measured
by timelines, deadlines, full agendas and so on. The emphasis is on
production, deliverables, end-product, output, consumables – all the
things that have us racing against the clock in an unnatural and
unhealthy way.

Most of us work best in our 'own time'. One person may be more productive in the morning, another person more productive at night. As
time is fundamentally our own, the quality of our time is also by nature
very personal. We make sacrifices when we put quantity before quality,

and while it may be difficult to admit it, we all quietly feel the exasperation of a quantity-first approach to time. If we tend to see time only as a unit measurement, we are seeing only a fraction of its value – and we lose a great deal of its potential value to us.

Ironically this applies to most things in life – we don't judge the worth of an art gallery by the number of paintings it has but by their quality. A good speech isn't more captivating because it is long – in fact, length can have the opposite effect. Similarly, a film can span centuries in the space of an hour and a half, but if it runs to epic length, it risks losing the audience.

Placing the emphasis consciously on quality helps us make more of our time. It helps us create time, get more out of it and use it as an energy in our life rather than an abstract idea that has no connection or relevance to our experience. It also helps us to be aware of our surroundings and the subtleties of life.

Panchang astrology places the emphasis on the quality of the moment, knowing that in each moment lies a powerful seed of potential. It emphasizes a balance between doing and being, creating and consuming, quality and quantity.

Much of our struggle with time can be alleviated by consciously looking at the quality of time and harmonizing our actions with its nature. Time in one sense is supreme – it moves according to divine laws. Moving with the flow of time means using the force of time to empower your actions. There is a lot to be gained by working with time quality rather than against it.

Think about it

More is not always better. It is always the quality of the moment that counts, not the quantity of time.

Give it a try

☾ Think of a time when a speech was too long, when a film dragged on or when a friend outstayed their welcome.

☾ What very brief moment of time has counted in a big way in your life?

PANCHANG IS TO TIME AS **FENG SHUI** IS TO SPACE

There exists ... space which is eternal and indestructible, which provides a position for everything that comes to be. Plato, *Timaeus*

Many of us have experienced that magical moment of being 'at the right place at the right time'. It is easy for us to think of the importance of the right **place**, less so when it comes to the right **time**. The physical reality of place is sensory and obvious. We can touch, smell, hear, taste and see what's in our space. And while what's in our space happens at a certain time, we do not normally attribute an influence to the time, except as a social or historical era, or a date to mark the moment of an action or event.

Time is more elusive than space. It's not something that's easily touched, tasted or seen. To say that it has quality may seem too much of an abstraction to those people who like to grasp reality in their fist. It is easier for us to put the emphasis on space. We know when we inhabit a nice space. We feel it. 'Location, location, location' says it all. Whether it's for work or pleasure, the quality of our space influences our experience. That's why the Chinese art of **feng shui** has gained a great deal of credence, even in the usually more conservative world of business. The BBC, for instance, has used **feng shui** consultants to help organize its head offices to enhance creativity, communication and general success. We believe in the use of **feng shui** because it is easy to experience the difference between spaces that are harmonically arranged and those that are left to random chaos. **Feng shui** does make sense, especially when the principle of cosmic harmony on which it is based is understood.

Einstein's General Theory of Relativity establishes that time and space have no independent reality – there exists only a kind of union of the two, which Einstein called 'space-time'.

The concept of a cosmic harmony is expressed in many ancient cultures, not least of which is India. Through their meditations, divine realizations and empirical observations, the Vedic sages understood the natural harmony of life. They gave expression to many of these ideas in original and deep ways. The **Isopanisad** describes the universe as consisting of an elaborate series of interconnected whole, perfect and complete units and sub-systems of units – an idea which is echoed in contemporary theories of quantum physics.

To the physicist, time and space are inseparable. You can't have one without the other. Any condition, event or being must exist simultaneously in both. To the Vedic sage both are interwoven in such a way that in principle the quality that exists in space is a reflection of the quality that exists in time – especially when it comes to action, cause and effect, and experience.

Space-time

The idea of a linear time in which events occur in succession is rejected by modern physics. The description of time according to quantum physics is surprisingly similar to the ancient concept of time. In de Broglie's words:

'Space and time cease to possess an absolute nature ... In space-time, everything which for each of us constitutes the past, the present, and the future is given in block, and the entire collection of events, successive for us, which form the existence of a material particle is represented by a line, the world-line of the particle.

Each observer, as his time passes, discovers, so to speak, new slices of space-time which appear to him as successive aspects of the material world, though in reality the ensemble of events constituting space-time exist prior to his knowledge of them.'

To the Vedic sages it was as important to harmonize your time as to harmonize your space. In their view you could not do one without the other, and of the two, time was considered more powerful. It made no sense to create an aesthetically pleasing and harmonious space at a discordant, chaotic or inauspicious time. Doing so would imbue the space with an attendant negative quality or vibration that would be at odds with an auspicious spatial arrangement. So the art of **Vashtu**, the Vedic version of **feng shui**, could only be effectively practised if the spatial construction were implemented at the right time and taking into consideration the unique needs and character of the client.

The combined arts of Panchang and **Vashtu** touched every aspect of life for thousands of years. Palaces, temples, homes and cities were all constructed at the right time and in accordance with the principles of **Vashtu**, while Panchang astrology was used to schedule almost anything of importance.

However, just as **feng shui** cannot in itself guarantee success, neither is Panchang a panacea for all ills or wants. With it one can create a suitable and pleasant stage on which to live, but of course one must then do the living and fill the space with happy and valuable experiences. In other words, one must still **act**.

Time, however, offers opportunity. Its plentiful, cyclical and regular qualities give us the chance to fill our lives with experience that enriches us in a deep way. Panchang is a tool that helps us aim for that enrichment both spiritually and materially.

Think about it

Think of how the time in which you live has influenced social trends and events and affected your experience of life.

Think back 5 years, 10 years, 15 years. What were you doing? Which times were your happiest or most difficult? How did your experience of life affect your life decisions?

Give it a try

)) Choose a day for this awareness exercise. Notice how the prevailing trends influence how you spend your time during the day. Consider how the time in which you live is influencing your choices in transport, leisure, work, relationships, fashion, politics, entertainment, technology, communication, travel, world-view and so on.

Quantum theory tells us that time is inseparable from space, although this has in large measure failed to translate into any practical guidance in terms of our use of time.

Science has also offered significant advances in slicing and dicing time into billionths of a second. IBM's new one-off £100M super computer will compute a billion million instructions in a second.[3] Physicists define the smallest 'meaningful' measure of time as 'Planck time' – the time it takes a photon travelling at the speed of light to cross the distance equal to Planck length, which is equal to 10^{-43} (written as 10 followed by 43 zeros).

3   *The Economist,* '2001: The Year in Review'

THE RIPPLE EFFECT

What goes around, comes around. Anonymous

Einstein's ultimate vision was that every part of the universe is linked to every other part of the universe. Nothing exists in isolation; everything exists in harmonious interaction with everything else. In other words, the principle of cause and effect runs at the very deepest level of the cosmos, creating the sophisticated matrix that we perceive as 'reality'. As space and time are intertwined, Nature's Law means that every action brings an equal and opposite reaction, and doing the right action at the right time creates right action. The Vedas called this karma.

Action and reaction are part of nature. For every action there is an equal and opposite reaction. We experience this in almost every aspect of our lives on a daily basis. Sometimes we are aware of it, sometimes not. It's a part of physics, but it's more than science. The principle of cause and effect touches even the most subtle parts of our being. How we think also affects the outcome of our actions. All action has its root in consciousness.

The Universe as Consciousness

This idealistic trend in modern physics goes back at least to the twin revolutions of relativity and quantum theory. In fact, of the dozen or so pioneers in these early revolutions – individuals such as Albert Einstein, Werner Heisenberg, Erwin Schrödinger, Louis de Broglie, Max Planck, Wolfgang Pauli, Sir Arthur Eddington – the vast majority of them were transcendentalists of one variety or another. And I mean that in a rather strict sense. From de Broglie's assertion that 'the mechanism demands a mysticism' to Einstein's Sponozist pantheism, from Schrödinger's Vedanta idealism to Heisenberg's Platonic archetypes: these pioneering physicists were united in the belief that the universe simply does not make sense – and can not be satisfactorily explained – without the inclusion, in some profound way, of consciousness itself.

'The universe begins to look more like a great thought than a great machine,' as Sir James Jeans summarized the available evidence. And, using words that virtually none of these pioneering physicists would object to, Sir James pointed out that it looks more and more certain that the only way to explain the universe is to maintain that it exists 'in the mind of some eternal spirit'.

Ken Wilber, *The Eye of Spirit*

To the Vedic sages, life's culmination was divine love, but they also knew that this attainment was rare, special and usually took time. There were many steps along the way. These were set out in the Vedas and related literature. In essence these works became manuals of action for the path to divinity, outlining stages on the journey which in the sages' eyes contained all manner of perfections and attainments, both material and spiritual.

In laying out this transcendent framework, the sages' view was practical. They understood that if they worked in a harmonious way with nature, they could live long, healthy and contented lives.

The Vedic sages understood the subtle mechanics of cause and effect and broadly described it as *karma*. The Sanskrit word *karma* means 'action' or 'activity'. In a sense karma is a generic word because in the Vedas different kinds are described – **a-karma, su-karma, vi-karma** – all representing a quality of action that creates a result of corresponding quality. There is **a-karma,** or unconscious actions that give bad results and which bring pain, loss and trouble. **Su-karma** is action that consciously brings good results and a wide range of benefits. **Vi-karma** is action which is wilfully destructive, even evil. The sages offered these descriptions with the aim of benefiting others by helping them avoid negative conditions, as well as guiding them to actions that would increase prosperity, knowledge and advancement in all areas of life.

A basic wisdom in this is that knowledge breeds knowledge, good begets good. In simple terms this is the universal 'prosperity principle'. Harmony breeds harmony. Stability creates stability. This knowledge has its root in consciousness, which the Vedic sages advanced through meditation and yoga. In their eyes, transcendence facilitated all things. Their view was holistic – material prosperity could serve the interests of spiritual awareness, and this could then bring balance, harmony and higher value to material actions and conditions. Both had the same origin and one could serve the other as long as all aspects of life were balanced and harmonious.

Panchang astrology was a practical tool that helped the sages work in harmony with nature. They guided their important efforts in a way that would create the least amount of friction to the natural divine order. In other words, they sought to reduce the effects of negative karma by using the knowledge of time quality to help transcend the troubles of the material world and reach higher states of enlightenment. They harmonized their action with the quality of time and aligned auspicious work with auspicious times. In doing so they harmonized their interaction with matter and eventually eliminated the ripple effect, the natural law of cause and effect, and advanced their lives in material and spiritual ways. By acting in harmony with time we too generate less friction and cause fewer disharmonious ripples in our environment.

Live simply that others may simply live.

Mahatma Gandhi

By acting in accordance with the greater scheme of things we can create harmony in our environment and bring peace and stability into our lives. When we act doesn't determine when we will see the outcome of that action, but there will be a ripple. What goes round comes around, and in due course we will experience the reaction to our action.

Consider the notion that everything you do affects everything else. Everything is connected to everything else. Energy cannot be destroyed, so the consequences of your thoughts and actions are never lost.
Remembering this creates more responsible action.
This means a better world in the future.

Time is the supreme Law of nature.

Sir Arthur Eddington, *Space, Time and Gravitation*

Think about it

Every time you have a cup of coffee or eat a bar of chocolate, someone picked the bean. Their land grows our luxuries instead of their staple foods. Were they paid enough to feed their family? Does their village have a school and a clean water supply?

Do you leave lights on when the room is empty? Do you leave your computer on overnight? In the UK the output of an entire electricity plant is required to keep electrical appliances on stand-by. Environmentalists are now saying that global warming is accelerating to such a point that temperatures are expected to rise by five degrees in the next 100 years. A temperature increase of two degrees, anticipated in 30 years' time, will be enough to melt the polar ice caps and cause devastating floods.

Give it a try

- ☾ Create a positive ripple effect in your environment. Consciously buy fair trade tea and coffee (and chocolate) in your next weekly shop. The growers are guaranteed an income to enable them to sustain their community.

- ☾ Switch off appliances when you have finished with them and replace hall security lights with low-energy light bulbs – they use a fraction of the energy.

- ☾ Use your time and energy consciously to create your future.

WORK IN
HARMONY
WITH TIME

Swim with the Current

Better to bend than to break. Scottish proverb

Time is greater than all of us – we are in it, part of it and smaller than it. It is a formidable natural force and deserves to be approached with humility and awareness. Time is the fabric of life. To use it well means offering it the same respect we offer to anything in nature – the sea, mountains, air, fire.

There is a difference between working with respect for Nature and having the will to conquer Her. It is sensible to swim with the current, sail with the wind – co-operate rather than dominate. When we work in harmony with nature we get good results, if not we don't. Feeding herbivore cattle animal offal, creating the BSE/CJD crisis and threat to human health, is one good example.

So making the best use of time means working in harmony with it. When we act in tune with the quality of time, our actions are supported by nature. Like a sailor who works **with** the wind, sea and tides, our efforts then have a life-giving potency.

Natural cycles affect all of us, it is just a question of how far we recognize it. Look around you and look inside yourself. As you grow in awareness of time and its quality you will be able to recognize its nature and influence. You will feel it in yourself and will see it in others. It is subtle, but then so is the air scented by a rose – you know it's there, but can't quite touch it.

The quality of time may appear delicate and easy and seem to give a sweet flow to the day's events, or it may be chaotic, unstable and challenging, a time when everything unravels and it is difficult to even find your keys. Whatever the quality of the moment, we all experience it.

DOING THE RIGHT THING AT THE RIGHT TIME TAKES LESS EFFORT

The gem cannot be polished without friction, nor man perfected without trials. Chinese proverb

We have sought to harness the power of nature since the beginning of time. Our most elegant inventions often use nature's power in simple but effective ways that minimize or eliminate the need for attention. Irrigation, the water wheel, the windmill, solar energy, fertilization, fermentation – the list is endless. The essence of any good engineering is to use the power inherent in a material or property – such as tensile strength, conduction or porousness – and have it do the work. The inherent quality of any moment in time can also be harnessed to a purpose.

Seeds sown in the spring, for example, take advantage of the season's energy. Sowing in another season requires more effort and facility, a greenhouse, lighting, ventilation. Bad timing – more effort. Good timing – less effort. Working with nature helps us conserve energy and resources and brings fewer problems. It pays to work with what's on offer. Using the energy and quality of time involves less effort and brings fewer complications.

To every thing there is a season,
and a time to every purpose under the heaven:

A time to be born, and a time to die; a time to plant,
and a time to pluck up that which is planted;

A time to kill, and a time to heal; a time to break down,
and a time to build up;

A time to weep, and a time to laugh; a time to mourn,
and a time to dance;

A time to cast away stones,
and a time to gather stones together;

A time to embrace, and a time to refrain from embracing;

A time to get, and a time to lose; a time to keep,
and a time to cast away;

A time to rend, and a time to sew; a time to keep silence,
and a time to speak;

A time to love, and a time to hate; a time of war,
and a time of peace.

Ecclesiastes 3:1–8

Choosing the Right Time

To choose time is to save time. Francis Bacon

Time means movement and for us a choice of action. Every action has its own unique characteristic, its own mixture of natural qualities that make it what it is. Each action also has specific qualities – writing poetry is imaginative, building work requires practicality, accountancy takes concentration, business involves risk, and so on.

Like time, every action is made up of the three modes of nature mentioned earlier: **sattva**, stability, **rajas**, industry, and **tamas**, apathy. Every action can be expressed differently according to the nature of the time and the awareness of the person. Take giving to charity as an example. Giving can be done with true generosity, which is **sattva**, with the expectation of reward and recognition, which is **rajas**, or without consideration of the value or righteousness of the cause, which is **tamas**. These three modes combine to produce specific natures of time and action.

To use time effectively we should be aware of its suitability for any type of action, just as we usually dress according to the nature of our action. Galas and dinner parties require black tie, the beach a swim-suit, hiking calls for walking boots, gardening a pair of overalls. Fashion serves a purpose. So do time and action.

Think about it

Recognize that there are times when it is best to act and times when it is wiser to wait.

Give it a try

☾ Be sensitive to your surroundings. What are they telling you? Do you feel it's a good time to act?

☾ Do you tend to act spontaneously and if so, do you normally get good results?

START AT
THE RIGHT TIME

The beginning is the half of every action.

Greek proverb

The day that starts bad, ends bad.

Old Mexican saying

Anything born in the moment of time carries
the quality of that moment.

Carl Jung

Get Off to a Good Start

The potential outcome of any action lies in its beginning, its conception, its initiation. Beginnings capture the essence of the moment, and the quality of that moment imbues the action with a direction, momentum and energy. The nature of the start determines the nature of the outcome.

Each moment has its own nature, which may or may not be compatible with the nature of the action and the person performing the action. Well-timed action considers the nature of the moment, the appropriateness of the action and whether the time suits the person. When these three conditions are positive, an action has the greatest support.

Good timing depends on the time of the start, not whether the entire action is performed during a positive period. Some actions will take a good deal of time to implement – building a business, a project, a house. The most important time is the beginning – signing the papers of incorporation, paying a fee to begin the project or laying the cornerstone of the building. The foundation stone of the Capitol building of the United States in Washington, for instance, was laid in pomp and ceremony at an astrologically auspicious time. It seems the Founding Fathers had the idea that beginning at a good time was a good investment in the future.

Starting at the right time does not mean that you can ignore everything else, however. Even if you set sail at the right time, it doesn't mean that you can neglect navigation, weather conditions or the sea-worthiness of the ship. The time quality itself may help the voyage to be smooth, but effort, patience, determination, discipline and ability are all required to ensure safe arrival in harbour.

MAKE THE
BEST OF
DIFFICULT TIMES

When you come to a roadblock, take a detour.

Mary Kay Ash

Time quality is constantly in flux. Like the sea, there is an ebb and flow. Like the sky, there is constant change, interplay of light and dark, cloud and sunshine. There are better and worse times just in a day and major shifts in time period over a week or month. In this flow of time we will inevitably encounter difficult and uncomfortable moments. When we do, it is best to make every effort to get the most out of them through action, not inaction.

This is simply being practical. It will not do to say to your boss, 'Oh, I am sorry I can't do my job today because it's a bad day.' The demands of daily life always pressure us into action. The important thing is to try to use the best times to set really important actions in motion. And if we must do something important on a day which has a disruptive nature, then at least we should try to use the best time that day to start.

Inevitably, of course, there will be times when we have no choice but to act, whatever the time quality. Taken in the right way this can be nature's message to us, helping us understand how things work in our world. We simply cannot control everything. When circumstances demand action at a bad time, at least we can be aware of what we are dealing with. Panchang is something like a weather forecast. Bad weather doesn't stop us going out, but when we do venture out we go prepared, with waterproof clothes or at least an umbrella. Watching a weather forecast helps you plan. If you know it is going to rain, rather than planning a picnic, you go for a coffee instead. Adjustment may be needed, but being flexible helps us interact with our environment in a powerful way.

If you know that the time ahead will be challenging, you are better prepared to rise to the challenges. For instance if the nature of time is stressful to communication, you will not be surprised by any misunderstandings and can adjust your tactics accordingly. Making an effort to communicate clearly will help you get through to people, even when conditions may be at their most difficult.

Also, if you have a difficult job to do, one that requires energy, focus and grit, a time that is by nature challenging can be harnessed productively. It's something like a double negative making a positive in grammar. A difficult time can be used to hit difficult matters head on. Challenging times can be used to break down obstacles and break through challenges – which is a vital part of regeneration and growth.

Panchang is not about finding the path of least resistance. It's not an excuse for procrastination or avoidance. Rather it's about understanding the nature and value of any day, accepting it and working with it.

It is helpful to emulate the nature of water when meeting obstacles. The nature of water is quiet insistence. Water knows no obstacles – it tends to flow around problems. This is the most effective way to realize your goals – rather than wasting energy on battling or attempting to move obstacles in your path, flow round them.

I like to think that the moon is there even if I am not looking at it. Einstein

The Moon's Primordial Power

Rains, floods, harvest, fertility – the Moon's primordial power is so obvious, but so little understood. In astrology, the Moon represents passivity, fertility, receptivity, woman, dreams, night and moistness. The most obvious effect of the Moon is on the tides. When the Sun's gravity augments the Moon's – at Full Moon and New Moon – the tides are at their highest.

But the Moon's influence reaches far beyond the tides. According to a recent study at Leeds University, there is a 3.6 per cent increase in visits to local GPs a few days after a Full Moon – equivalent to 30,000 extra visitors nationally per cycle.[4] Various studies have also shown that mental patients tend to become more disturbed on Full Moon days.[5] Many police officers will swear to an increase in violent crime, murder and arson during Full Moons. Nurses, medical staff and health professionals say there is a surge in accidents and admissions to mental hospitals and casualty departments.[6]

Obstetricians tend to believe that pregnant women are more likely to deliver during Full Moons than at other times in the Lunar cycle. Some studies have demonstrated these connections,[7] but many others have not, and so the topic remains steeped in controversy.

4   *Daily Mail*, 13 December 2000. A research team at Leeds University headed by Dr Neal studied the effects of 12 Full Moons on 60 practices. Dr Neal's study is published in the medical journal *Family Practice*.

5   See for instance, 'Lunacy revisited: the influence of the moon on mental health and quality of life', *Journal of Psychosocial Nursing*, May 2000. This new study reports findings from an analysis of 100 mentally ill people over a 30-month period. The results show a significant change at the time of the Full Moon in patients suffering from schizophrenia. Many hospitals rota extra medical staff for psychiatric wards and accident and emergency departments around the Full Moon.

6   A 1995 study at the University of New Orleans asked 325 subjects whether Lunar phenomena altered people's behaviour (D. E. Vance, 'Belief in lunar effects on human behaviour', *Psychol. Rep.* 76 (1), 1995, 32–4). They found that 43 per cent of the people surveyed were convinced that it does. Those who believed this most strongly were mental health professionals, including social workers, clinical psychologists with master's degrees and nurse's aides. An earlier study, published in the *Journal of Emergency Medicine* in 1987, found that 80 per cent of emergency room nurses and 64 per cent of physicians believed the Moon affected their patients.

7 A FEW EXAMPLES:

Over a five-year period, 11,613 cases of aggravated assault: assaults occurred more often around the Full Moon (A. L. Lieber, 'Human aggression and the lunar synodic cycle', *J. Clin. Psychiatry* 39 (5), 1978, 385–92).

Over a one-year period, 34,318 crimes: crimes occurred more frequently during the Full Moon (*J. Psychology* 93, 1976, 81–3).

Over an 11-year period, the admission records of 18,495 patiets to a psychiatric hospital: admissions for psychosis were highest during the New Moon and lowest during the Full Moon (C. E. Climent and R. Plutchik, 'Lunar madness: an empirical study', *Compr. Psychiatry* 18 (4), 1977, 369–74).

Over a four-year period, 841 cases of 'self-poisoning': self-poisoning occurred more often on the day of the Full Moon (C. P. Thakur, R. N. Sharma and H. S. Akhtar, 'Full moon and poisoning', *Br. Med. J.* 281 (1980), 1,684).

Over a one-year period, calls to a poison centre: unintentional poisonings occurred more often during the Full Moon cycle; intentional poisonings (suicides/drug abuse) occurred more often at the New Moon (G. M. Oderda and W. Klein-Schwartz, 'Lunar cycle and poison centre calls', *J. Toxicol. Clin. Toxicol.* 20 (5), 1983, 487–95).

Pregnant women who have already had children were found to be significantly more likely to give birth on the day of a Full Moon (G. Ghiandoni, R. Secli, M. B. Rocchi and G. Ugolini, 'Incidence of lunar position in the distribution of deliveries: a statistical analysis', *Minerva Ginecol.* 49 (3), 1997, 91–4).

the eleven
qualities
of
time

What do we mean exactly by quality of time? The thousands of astrological conditions that symbolize innumerable subtle shifts in time qualities can be grouped into 11 different categories. With practice we can observe these in a tangible way. All 11 qualities of time originate in the three modes of nature – **sattva**, stability, **rajas**, industry, and **tamas**, entropy. Just as the three primary colours (red, blue and yellow) combine to create the basic colours green, orange, purple, brown, and so on, so the modes of nature combine to create 11 conditions of time quality. These further combine to create a wealth of subtle and gross influences and conditions, similar to how the various colours of a palette can be used to create paintings of diverse mood and effect.

The 11 qualities are: Tender, Light, Fixed, Swift, Fierce, Dreadful, Mixed; Increasing or Decreasing; and Supportive or Challenging.

The names symbolize the general nature of the time qualities. Tender has a gentle mood, Light has a frivolous touch, Swift is fast-paced, Fixed feels steady and solid, while Fierce brings focus, energy and direction, Dreadful brings a chaotic tendency and Mixed is a mixture of qualities. Each of these seven conditions lasts about a day and a half, though they can be followed by another of the same quality and last for up to three days at a time. The various qualities are symbolized by the constellations or **nakshatras** which the Moon passes through on its monthly course through the constellations of the zodiac.

The two major Lunar influences, Supportive or Challenging, blend with the seven natures and create a further depth of influence. These two are cornerstones of astrological time quality and are symbolized by the days of the Lunar cycle. A Lunar day is shorter than a Solar day and there are 15 Lunar days in each Lunar fortnight. Each day is either Supportive or Challenging by nature.

The Challenging Lunar days occur just before New Moon, just before Full Moon and at the Quarter Moons. With a couple of exceptions the Lunar days in between tend to be Supportive.

Increasing or Decreasing times correspond to the phases of the Moon and symbolize its influence on the creation or reduction of momentum in action. These phases tend to bring growth and expansion, or reduction, withdrawal and retreat.

The waxing cycle of the Moon is a good time for growth. Its energy suffuses action with an expansive dynamic and thus it is called Increasing. The waning Moon offers less energy as it decreases, in fact it tends to draw energy away as it slims and thus it is called Decreasing. It is more suited to routine chores and maintenance or clearing out and simplifying things, rather than making expansive plans.

The following chapters describe each of the qualities and natures. Later in the book we will show you how you can observe these in your environment, plan for them and use them effectively by matching them to activities that are important to you.

TENDER

Being kind to others is a way of being good to yourself. Rabbi Harold Kushner

The Tender nature of time is loving, nurturing, sensitive, thoughtful, understanding, compassionate, enlightening, gentle, sweet, artistic, creative, imaginative, supportive, succulent, expanding, progressive, auspicious, helpful, co-operative and inspired.

Tender time quality offers those special moments that are highly supportive and encouraging. In any Lunar month there are approximately four to five periods of time that are predominantly of this quality. They do not necessarily coincide with a full Solar or calendar day – it is possible that a day may start out with a Tender nature and end up with a different quality operating.

Tender times are good for doing anything that requires growth, development, empathy and agreeability. They are very good times for romance, starting relationships, forging new partnerships, laying the foundation of important projects, opening institutions (schools, hospitals, charities, etc), gardening, artistic and creative efforts, mediation, negotiating settlements, establishing peace and dealing with financial matters, including investment.

Tender time quality helps to create a fluid, agreeable and conducive environment. It smoothes communication, soothes sensitive feelings, enables collaboration, encourages closeness and intimacy, fosters understanding and heightens sensual and romantic exchanges. It is also supportive to the creation of prosperity, which is why it can be used for financial matters, and it forms a good basis for teamwork, the exchange of ideas and diplomatic efforts.

Tender times are not particularly powerful for adversarial or competitive actions, as they do not stimulate a competitive urge or sense of awe in an opponent. However, Tender times do not inhibit or restrict these efforts.

How it can feel

Soft, sweet, tender, pampering, attentive, understanding, warm, fuzzy, loving, glowing, indulgent, easy-going, upbeat, open. In certain circumstances, for instance when you feel low in energy, you may feel emotionally vulnerable.

How you recognize it

Events and efforts tend to flow smoothly. Interactions are positive and jovial. There is an openness in exchanges with others. Help and encouragement are at hand. There is a general generosity of spirit, receptivity to ideas and empathy in dealings.

LIGHT

The universe is full of magical things
patiently waiting for our wits to grow
sharper. Eden Phillpotts

Light times are quite subtle, airy, delicate and ephemeral and tend to be positive, upbeat, uplifting, inspirational, thought-provoking, stirring, mischievous, humorous, prankish, decorative, flirtatious and expressive.

Light time periods are a little more energetic than Tender times. Light time quality is literally 'lighter' – more delicate, less substantial and sensory – than any of the other time qualities.

Light times are good for anything that requires energy, openness, growth, an exchange of ideas, knowledge, community and creativity. This is a very supportive time quality for social events, celebrations, communication, marketing, presentations, selling, business, education and instruction, the media, various campaigns, fashion, theatre, entertainment, playfulness, decoration and adornments, fashion, hairdressing and make-up, chatting, exchanging ideas, partying, socializing and just plain fun. It is also conducive to spiritual matters, meditation, reflection, daydreaming and reverie.

Light times help create an understanding based on the spirit of idea and principles. This is a very helpful time quality for all forms of communication. It stimulates pure creativity – although this may lack a practical basis or focus – and is helpful to the creation of prosperity, well-being, community benefit and charitable causes. New projects, businesses and creative efforts are all well supported by Light times, especially if the nature of the endeavour shares something in common with a Light time – for instance, media projects, marketing or team brainstorming. A Light time offers auspicious beginnings and can bring lasting effects.

Light times are not suited to serious business matters or detailed work requiring persistence or concentration. This is not a strong time for finalizing details, consolidating plans or making a commitment.

How it can feel

Enticing, compelling, festive, inspiring, abundant, frivolous, humorous, fleeting, expressive, subtle, hopeful, insubstantial.

How you recognize it

It is pleasant. It lacks seriousness. There is an ease of exchange, plentiful ideas, a mood of exploration, reluctance for discipline, lack of worry, sense of adventure. People are happy and gossipy.

FIXED

Three people were at work on a construction site. All were doing the same job, but when each was asked what the job was, the answers varied. 'Breaking rocks,' the first replied. 'Earning my living,' the second said. 'Helping to build a cathedral,' said the third.   Peter Schultz

A Fixed time is grounded, long-lasting, solid, steady, strong, progressive, constructive, binding, earthy, unswerving, deeply rooted and steadfast.

Fixed time quality gives stability, purpose, direction and substance to action. It tends to offer focus and unobstructed vision of practical matters.

Fixed times are good for anything that requires dependability and reliability, including finance, banking, trade, construction, development, binding legal matters such as contracts and agreements, political unions, founding governments and trusts, incorporating companies, the purchase of land, buildings or houses, concluding negotiations, mining, mechanical work, accounting and engineering.

Fixed times create a solid foundation for almost any effort. This time quality supports work that requires gradual development, incremental growth and the achievement of long-range objectives. It is especially good for work where you do not require immediate or short-term results, as this time quality has a tendency to be rather plodding, bringing steady progress rather than swift results.

Fixed times help create a sense of trust, reliability and a pulling together of team or group efforts, especially larger groups. They can help significantly to create prosperity through land, real estate, long-term deposits, bonds, stocks, antiques and precious objects.

Fixed times can also lead to a sense of boredom or being 'stuck in a rut' without the restlessness to do something about it. Matters can seem routine and rather dull. If your energy level is low, it will be diffi-cult to come up with bright ideas or innovative solutions during a Fixed time. Relationships can slow down or lose their sparkle and one or other person may feel taken for granted.

How it can feel

Steady, calm, settled, contented, straightforward, unexciting, 'normal', slow, boring in a good kind of way, unaffected, undisturbed.

How you recognize it

It is calm, reassuring, uneventful. There is a focus on work and productivity, on making steady progress. Things run automatically. It's business as usual.

SWIFT

If you chase two rabbits, both will escape. Anonymous

Swift accurately describes the essential nature of this time quality. Swift times are dynamic, energetic, full of movement, momentum, passion, force and vitality. They can bring inspiration, direction, a sense of urgency, a need to act, nervousness, a mild touch of chaos, disorientation, clarity through action and movement, and serendipity.

Swift times are good for anything that requires energy, swift action, speed, purpose, communication, short-term results and rapid progress. They have a wide range of uses, both positive and negative, although it is important to understand that there is an element of instability to Swift times, just as a fast-moving vehicle can easily go off course without a careful driver at the wheel.

Swift times are good for any type of personal or organizational communication, social work, media activity, public relations (the time should be suited to the person for whom the work is being done), conferences, meetings, presentations, negotiations where a quick settlement is desired, business, trade, industry, transport, travel, shipping, dispatches, political action, networking, mass action, marketing, short-term financial trading and transactions, and debate (especially if it's a powerful time for the debater). Swift times are also well suited to setting out on journeys, especially if you want to return quickly having achieved your goals, as with short business trips.

Swift times create a dynamic, spontaneous, reactive and impulsive energy that is a good medium for anything related to ideas, passion, principles, information and education. This time quality is very conducive to most communications efforts, although it can create misunderstandings when details are overlooked. This can also happen when an audience is swept away by the force and vigour of a presentation but fails to realize the deeper meaning behind it.

Swift times are very good for teamwork, emergency communication, urgent diplomacy and crisis management. However, the person who is likely to be best able to manage this energy is someone who is structured and focused, but who also enjoys the adrenaline that can rise with the appearance of a Swift time. Otherwise it is possible to feel a loss of energy from keeping up with a Swift time quality. This can make one feel depleted or exhausted. The trick is to use the energy without being overwhelmed by it. Keeping centred in a Swift time is essential for effectiveness.

How it can feel

Busy, hectic, inspired, purposeful, directed. There is a sense of urgency, of high energy, of being carried along by events, of a second wind of energy you didn't know you had.

How you recognize it

There is an increase of activity, a frenzy, a tendency to action, an increase in communications (phone calls, faxes, e-mails, etc), a sudden change of direction, a change in attitude, brisk trade, sudden arrangements, new information, excitement, a sense of momentum, infectious positivism. Journeys will proceed at pace, without delay, although you run the risk of double-booking appointments or missing a train as you are swept along by the high energy.

May you travel with the wind at your back.

Native American saying

FIERCE

Obstacles cannot crush me. Every obstacle yields to stern resolve. He who is fixed to a star does not change his mind. Leonardo da Vinci

Fierce time qualities are sharp, cutting, intense, focused, penetrating, piercing, forceful, energetic, purposeful, directed, wilful, driven and driving, challenging, polemical, combative and competitive.

The name 'Fierce' sounds a touch gothic and can at first evoke reactions of fear and concern. However, the names of the time qualities symbolize a wide range of influences that can manifest in many of life's portfolios. So take them as indicative of these influences and don't jump to conclusions about any Fierce or Dreadful time quality being extreme or destructive. Fierce is not a bad description for this influence, although it can be very creative and constructive in its own special way.

Fierce time has a wide range of practical and productive uses. We can understand how it works by looking to any process of growth in nature, which is almost always preceded by an absorption of life force or breaking down to create fertile compost for new growth. Seasons are a perfect example, where the winter is a time of hidden regeneration before the spring's birthing energy. So friction, resistance, tension, force and argument all have a positive use. Some type of force is required in most creative processes, whether in birth, sculpture, building projects or redecoration. The preparation inevitably involves some dismantling of the old to make way for the new.

Fierce times are strong for anything that requires intensity, high energy, force, will, determination, breakthrough, grit, abrasion, and growth through change or challenge. Fierce times are in fact very productive. Also, having advance knowledge that a time is Fierce helps remove the uncertainty and tension that we would normally experience during its influence, and enables us to use the time constructively.

Fierce times are good for breaking down barriers, pushing through personal and group limits, research, investigative work, dealing with challenging or difficult issues, cutting through red tape and bringing a high degree of concentrated energy to projects. Fierce times can be put to good use in business and financial matters, selling and marketing, competitive sports, campaigns, stock trading, competition, debate, military and police action, construction, demolition, renovation and reorganization. On a simple daily level a Fierce time quality is excellent for hard work, clearing uncompleted tasks, filing and doing accounts.

If handled with a focused consciousness, a Fierce time can be a powerful catalyst for development and change. If used or experienced from an imbalanced or emotional perspective, it can be over-forceful and break things unnecessarily.

How it can feel

Sharp, intense, focused, decisive, energetic, edgy, probing, intrusive, disruptive, challenging, disturbing, revealing, surprising, abrupt, abrasive, combative.

How you recognize it

It creates uncertainty and brings up difficult issues that need attention and that we would rather avoid. It also brings clarity and focus in your intention, energy and direction from others, sharpness in exchanges, challenges and confrontations that turn constructive, emotional expression, actions that appear aggressive, misunderstanding in dealings, people being overbearing and the triumph of strong over the weak.

DREADFUL

In all chaos there is cosmos, in all disorder a secret
order.   Carl Jung

Dreadful times are chaotic, unstable, disturbing, disruptive, **apparently**
disharmonious, harsh, aggressive, unsettled and unsettling, and they
can be unpleasant, raw, crude, wild and brutal.

Of all the time qualities Dreadful, as the name implies, is the most
challenging and disruptive. Still, it can be useful in many ways to
someone who has learned to 'bend with the wind' of time quality. Also,
it is rare to experience a **purely** Dreadful time quality that is not
modified or ameliorated by other qualities.

There are times, however, when life does appear to be harsh and to
lack empathy. Empathy is fundamental to healthy relationships and is
the hallmark of a progressive and ethical character. In the absence of
empathy even the other virtues seem brutal. Seen from a higher perspective, or from a more informed view, there is usually a purpose to
the harsher moments in life. But it often takes some time, distance and
wisdom to understand them.

Dreadful time qualities are recognizable by their generally chaotic and
disruptive nature. They also have a subtle aspect that is usually best

observed with hindsight. For instance a Dreadful time quality can influence a conflict whose consequences may take time to appear.

Dreadful times can be used productively for anything that requires transformation, regeneration through breaking resistance, letting go of anything outmoded and useless, implementing important changes, plumbing the depths of an issue, radical revaluation or the conquering of inner and outer foes. Dreadful times are good for dealing with recalcitrance, aggressive competition, high-energy sports, investigations, litigation, placing a challenge, scrapping material, demolition, bringing problems to light, confrontation, police work, divestiture, litigation, some business dealings, such as defending against aggressive takeover bids, and difficult issues in general.

Dreadful times tend to be nature's way of stirring things up. They are Her catalyst for change. Working co-operatively with nature during these times can help us get the best from them. The Vedas tell us that the best way to approach a Dreadful time period is with detachment and the understanding that everything is subject to change and that breaking barriers creates progress. The knowledge that change makes way for growth is also helpful in managing Dreadful time quality. Some people even enjoy this kind of time quality and get a thrill from the challenge and adrenaline it tends to bring.

On a practical note, Dreadful times are especially unsuitable for marriage, property dealings, the initiation of new partnerships, travel and harmonious romantic affairs.

How it can feel

Chaotic, disruptive, confrontational, explosive, turbulent, angry, discordant, unnerving. It can generate a sense of fear, agitation, worry or irritation, an urge to react or lash out, or a desire to run away, hide or escape from a conflict.

How you recognize it

There is uncertainty, discord, tension, suspicion, anger, frustration, misunderstanding, disunity, sudden change, confrontation, discontinuity and a lack of co-operation.

MIXED

The art of progress is to preserve
order amid change and to preserve
change amid order. Alfred North Whitehead

For nothing is fixed, forever and forever and forever,
it is not fixed; the earth is always shifting, the light is
always changing, the sea does not cease to grind
down rock. Generations do not cease to be born,
and we are responsible to them because we are the
only witnesses they have. The sea rises, the light
fails, lovers cling to each other, and children cling to
us. The moment we cease to hold each other, the
sea engulfs us and the light goes out. James Baldwin

Mixed time qualities have an intensity about them. They are energetic but in a subtle, understated way, gentle but with a sharp edge, robust but somewhat passive, disruptive but in a positive way and penetrating in a tender manner.

It is misleading to think of a Mixed time quality as being an amalgam of all the other qualities, because Mixed implies the changing and exchanging of energies in time. The various qualities change subtly and frequently. So a Mixed Lunar day may have at its beginning a predominance of Fixed quality but then change to become more Fierce in nature.

It may be helpful to think of Mixed quality times as a swirl of colour. Pour red, yellow and blue into a bucket and stir the mixture with a stick and you will get purple, orange and green, all in different shades and mixes. Mixed time quality has a similar nature.

We all have the experience of coming home and saying, 'Ugh, was that a mixed bag of a day' or something like that. Maybe you went to work and missed your bus, but being late to work meant you missed a bomb scare, you found a £50 note on the seat and you finally got the chance to talk to the girl in accounts for the first time.

Mixed time qualities can be used in creating something positive by accepting limits and challenges. Mixed time periods are also good for efforts where you can be flexible in terms of the final outcome.

Mixed time qualities are, however, the least reliable of the time qualities in terms of giving definitive outcomes. They have an unpredictable element that can give varying results. In one sense Mixed times are more dependent on the condition of a person's astrological chart and the conditions in which that person is operating. They also occur less frequently in a Lunar cycle than any of the other time qualities.

How it can feel

Routine, somewhat uneventful, tenuous, sensitive, receptive and yet uncertain and potentially changeable.

How you recognize it

Mixed is probably the most difficult of the time qualities to observe in your environment. Like a day of sunny spells and scattered showers, with clouds scudding across the sky, the mixture of influences may be in turn positive but challenging, disruptive but constructive. There may be directed effort but uncertain outcome and a sense of purpose and well-being but an element that is sharp and discordant.

INCREASING

These seven qualities of time set the predominant mood of the day. They can be expressed with greater or lesser intensity and may be quite subtle or very obvious. This depends on other astrological factors. The fabric of time may be either Challenging or Supportive and the momentum of the time may be either Increasing or Decreasing.

Increasing momentum encourages growth, expansion, development, awareness, enhancement, multiplication and longevity. It lends strength, support, vitality, energy and vigour to any action and amplifies the effects of the previous seven time qualities. It infuses time with a progressive quality, adding a force or push to any action, giving it the benefit of a wave of energy that tends to grow as time goes on.

Wherever possible, it is desirable to initiate important actions and large projects during an Increasing time quality. An Increasing time is especially helpful to strategic efforts. It is very well suited to travel, business, education, investment, house purchase, business incorporation, the laying of a cornerstone – any important action whose effect will be long-lasting.

Increasing times are generally supportive, but tend to amplify the other time qualities in operation. So a Tender time quality during an Increasing time period will give good results in time, but a Dreadful time quality during an Increasing period will tend to develop its challenging qualities as time goes on.

Increasing time qualities take their energy from the waxing phase of the Moon. A general guideline is to do the really important things during the waxing phase of the Moon. This lets you tap into the expanding energy and channel it into your efforts. In general it is a time for action, change and constructive development.

Moon Rise

There are $29^{1/2}$ days from Full Moon to Full Moon. Most diaries and calendars will show Full Moons and New Moons, but there is another way to tell whether the Moon is waxing or waning:

☾ If the sky is clear, all you have to do is look up.

☾ If you don't see the Moon, day or night, it's the time of the New Moon.

☾ If you see the Moon at night, it's waning – decreasing from Full Moon to New Moon.

☾ If you can see the Moon during the day, it's waxing – growing from New Moon to Full Moon.

☾ If it's the time of the Full Moon, the Moon will rise at sunset and you can't miss it.

Actions taken closer to the New Moon phase of the waxing Moon – the beginning of the Lunar cycle – will tend to bring results in the long term. The more closely strategic actions are taken to the Full Moon, the more momentum the quality of time carries with it and thus the results will tend to appear in the short term. However, the day prior to the Full Moon is highly unstable (see p.130).

Rule of Thumb

There is also a quick rule of thumb (literally) to find out whether the Moon is waxing or waning:

☾ Look at your thumbnail. You'll see a light pink crescent at its base.

☾ If the Moon looks like the crescent on your left thumb (a 'D' shape), it's a waxing Moon.

☾ If the Moon looks like the crescent of your right thumb (a 'C' shape), it's a waning Moon.

☾ This applies in the northern hemisphere. The rule works the opposite way around in the southern hemisphere.

Give it a try

☾ Find a monthly calendar that shows the phases of the Moon. In the morning and the evening make a mental note of the phase of the Moon, how you feel, what your experience of the day is and any major events that have happened.

☾ When the Moon is waxing, put more effort into new projects and creative endeavours.

☾ When the Moon is waning, tend to more routine matters.

☾ Make a note of your observations on how the Moon's phases affect you.

☾ If you can, make a point of looking at the Moon. Spend a few moments contemplating its symbolism and meaning. Think about how this meaning is naturally woven into your day-to-day life.

Waxing Moon Beauty Tips

☾ The waxing Moon is a good time to build up your physical strength or build up muscle.

☾ If you are trying to lose weight, avoid heavy, fatty or sweet foods, because your body is in an absorbent phase.

☾ If you want your hair to grow dense and long, cut it under a waxing Moon.

☾ This is a good time to take vitamins and mineral supplements.

DECREASING

Like this cup, you are full of your own opinions and speculations. How can I show you Zen unless you first empty your cup? Nan-in, Japanese master

Decreasing time qualities symbolize the cycles in nature and activity that are a vital part of regeneration. These are times when there is a gradual reduction in the pace of energy, which offers respite and a time of consolidation to all living things.

Decreasing time quality brings a lessening of momentum and dynamism. It tends towards withdrawal, introversion and consolidation. Decreasing time quality occurs during the waning Lunar fortnight. In the early part of the phase, immediately after the Full Moon, the time quality is still largely dynamic and tends to imbue action with a vibrancy and momentum. Due to its waning nature, however, the long-term trend of any action begun in this cycle is towards a gradual reduction in momentum and force.

The time from the twelfth Lunar day, approximately three days before the New Moon in the waning phase, until the New Moon is highly unstable and generally ill suited to important efforts that need stability and energy for sustained long-term growth. The energy at work at this time offers little support to anything conceived under its influence. This period is so recessive, unstable and low in energy that actions begun now are likely to be highly troublesome, unstable, even destructive in nature. It is therefore wise to avoid using this period, especially the day before the New Moon, for anything other than simple routine matters.

Actions started in the Increasing time quality will tend to give its results as time progresses, whereas those begun in the Decreasing quality will give them sooner – but they tend to give less in terms of abundance.

Decreasing times are suited to tactical matters, day-to-day efforts and routine work. They are ill suited to embarking on strategic efforts, but are good for strategic review, analysis and discussion – where you want to take an accurate assessment of a situation in a calm and collected manner. They are also good for introspection, taking stock, recharging your batteries, retreat, seclusion and meditation. Any activity where there is a desire for reduction and withdrawal is sup-ported during a Decreasing time.

Decreasing time qualities are well suited to routine business, mainte-nance, renovation, particularly any phase of work that removes structures, divestiture, planning, research, paying off debts and refi-nancing for debt reduction. The Decreasing fortnight is good for travel, although the last two days before the New Moon are highly unstable, which can cause disruption to plans. Diets, detoxi-fying and muscle-toning programmes are also supported by Decreasing time quality.

If your dreams turn to dust ... vacuum.

Waning Moon

☾ You can perform important tasks during the waning Moon,
but not those that require growth. This is a time for assessment
and learning from mistakes.

☾ Use the time to wind down and prepare for the next cycle of the Moon.

☾ Shed emotional baggage – anything that is cluttering your life.

☾ Don't start new ventures and don't buy a house during the
waning Moon.

☾ If you can, postpone important journeys.

☾ If you're winding down a project or company, or pruning a
team or committee, it's best to do it in the second half of the
Decreasing fortnight.

Waning Moon Detox Health Tips

☾ Use the days leading up to the New Moon to begin a fast and
kick bad habits such as smoking and drinking coffee. Toxins
are more easily released from the body at this time, which will
tend to make withdrawal symptoms less severe.

☾ This is an ideal time for detoxification, cleansing diets, losing weight, having surgery (bleeding is less severe) and making that long overdue visit to the dentist (plaque is more easily removed). It's also ideal for relaxing and taking it easy.

New Moon

☾ The New Moon is the tail end of a cycle, representing potential that is latent or hidden.

☾ Use this time to make plans, set your goals and express your desires. Use the New Moon day to prepare for the days ahead, but don't begin your important efforts yet. Focus on your inner needs and do some serious thinking about your goals.

☾ The day right after a New Moon is always good. This is an ideal time to put plans in motion – start a relationship, go after a new job.

☾ Projects put into action at the start of the waxing Moon will generally be imbued with stability and the potential for long-term growth.

SUPPORTIVE

Supportive and Challenging times qualities make up the basis of any day's general influence. They are the stage on which the other time qualities interact.

Supportive time qualities are generally stable, constructive, harmonious, positive, helpful and balanced. They offer a good foundation for growth, so almost any activity performed under their influence is helped. When mixed in the right way with the other time qualities, a Supportive time lends strength, durability, vibrancy, vigour and purpose to any action and encourages the desired results.

For example, when a Dreadful time is mixed with a Supportive time, the Supportive time offers a good opportunity for the Dreadful quality to be expressed constructively. Under this influence, even the 'negative' quality of a Dreadful time will bring good results in the end. The experience of such a mixture, while undoubtedly lively, will also tend to be positive.

CHALLENGING

Challenging time periods tend to occur just before the Full and New and on the Quarter Moons in both the Increasing (waxing) and Decreasing (waning) phases. They bring different degrees of difficulty and complication. Their nature is unstable and they tend to create discord.

The most difficult period is just before the New Moon, closely followed by the day before the Full Moon, with less destabilizing effects at the time of the Last Quarter of the waning Moon and First Quarter of the waxing Moon. There are other Challenging periods of a lesser intensity on the fourth, sixth, ninth and twelfth Lunar days, but their influence is more subtle and so harder to observe in the general environment.

Challenging Lunar days tend to be disruptive, unstable and problematic. They lack harmony and flow, and can be experienced as confusing, disturbing, chaotic and pinching. It is best to use these times for routine work, although they can be used quite well for creative work, breaking down barriers, research and constructive confrontation – if the person in question has a good measure of self-awareness, balance, empathy and personal control.

Challenging Lunar days are when the more emotional sides of our personalities are expressed, so if you tend to be passionate and angry, you should consciously temper your reaction to events going on around you at these times. A small touch of emotion or anger becomes exaggerated by the quality of time and can create reactions and difficulties disproportionate to the value of the original problem. In other words, these times make things seem much worse than they really are.

Using our analogy that Supportive and Challenging times are the stage on which the other qualities perform, Challenging times are a cramped stage that lacks structural stability or good lighting (the ability to see things in perspective), with confused or inconsistent direction, where no one can remember their lines or understand those of the other actors. In some cases the stage may be so weak that it wobbles, tipping the action to and fro. It doesn't make for a good performance.

The power of Panchang lies in knowing in advance when these times are operating. Through either conscious observation, intuition or recourse to astrological information such as is found at **www.panchang.com,** anyone can plan their time to get the most out of it, according to its quality and their own nature.

It could be argued that this is just one more thing to think about and manage. But we are dealing with these things anyway. Whether consciously or unconsciously, we must deal with these qualities of time as we deal with all the various factors in our lives. Time qualities are working on and within our environment.

The social psychologist Erich Fromm said that the very purpose of man is to become conscious. This is the Vedic view also. The more conscious we are, the more powerful we are and the greater freedom we have. Knowledge is power. This is why the Vedas offer Panchang as one of many tools that help us expand, hone and perfect our inner and outer awareness.

So far we have presented a very large set of astrological conditions. In the following three sections we will show you how to use these in a simple and practical way, mixing and matching time quality with your actions to get the most from your time.

EVERY DAY
IS A COMBINATION
OF QUALITIES

The 11 qualities of time form the palette from which an endless array of time quality is mixed. While the mixture may be subtle, even ephemeral, with practice it is possible to see the qualities' influence emerge in a definitive way.

Any day is a combination of three qualities – one taken from the three main types: Challenging or Supportive; Tender, Light, Fixed, Swift, Fierce, Dreadful and Mixed; and Increasing or Decreasing. Below is a list of combinations from the most positive to the most challenging. (At this point we do not consider whether a time is in harmony with your own astrological chart, which is another important factor in selecting good times.) The combinations are:

☾ **Supportive-Increasing-Tender/Light/Swift/Fixed**

☾ **Supportive-Increasing-Fierce/Mixed**

☾ **Supportive-Increasing-Dreadful**

☾ **Supportive-Decreasing-Tender/Light/Swift/Fixed**

☾ Supportive-Decreasing-Fierce/Mixed

☾ Supportive-Decreasing-Dreadful

☾ Challenging-Decreasing-Tender/Light/Swift/Fixed

☾ Challenging-Decreasing-Fierce/Mixed

☾ Challenging-Decreasing-Dreadful

☾ Challenging-Increasing-Tender/Light/Swift/Fixed

☾ Challenging-Increasing-Fierce/Mixed

☾ Challenging-Increasing-Dreadful

This illustrates how time qualities combine to produce a wide range of influences that are unique to each day.

We have made the selection of the above combinations easy for you at www.panchang.com. There you can 'surf the future' to see the quality of time at any day, time and place. There is also a powerful time quality search engine that lets you search for the best times for over 300 different types of activity. The last section of this book describes the various features of the site and how to use them (see p.197).

MATCHING TIME QUALITY AND ACTION TYPES

Previously we mentioned that actions have unique characteristics. In this section we offer a simple exercise that shows how you can match time qualities to different types of action.

Try to choose a suitable quality of time for the following activities:

1   Starting a muscle-toning exercise regime

2   Going on a diet

3   A wedding day

4   Setting out on an action holiday

5   Clearing out cupboards

6   Gardening:
     a)   for growth
     b)   for clearing, weeding and pruning

7   Sailing

8   Decorating:
        a)   for decorative paintwork/soft furnishings
        b)   for structural or practical building work

9   Singing/performing in the theatre

10   Starting a course to learn a new skill:
        a)   for creative work
        b)   for focused study and revision
        c)   for teamwork

11   Investigations and research

12   Investing in long-term bonds

13   Selling off under-performing shares

14   Taking legal action, suing for damages

15   Signing an employment contract

Answers to the above

1   Supportive-Increasing-Fixed

2   Supportive-Decreasing-Light/Swift

3   Supportive-Increasing/Decreasing-Tender/Fixed

4   Supportive-Increasing/Decreasing-Swift/Fierce

5   Challenging-Decreasing-Swift/Fierce/Dreadful

6a   For growth: Supportive-Increasing-Fixed/Tender/Light.
6b   For clearing, weeding and pruning: Supportive-Decreasing
        Fierce/Dreadful.

7   Supportive-Increasing or Decreasing-Swift/Tender/Light/Fixed/Fierce

8a   For decorative paintwork/soft furnishings: Supportive-
        Increasing/Decreasing-Tender/Light.
8b   For structural or practical building work: Fixed.

9   Supportive-Increasing/Decreasing-Tender/Light

10a   For creative skills: Supportive-Increasing-Tender/Light.
10b   For focused study and revision: Fierce or Fixed.
10c   For teamwork: Light.

11   Supportive or Challenging-Increasing or Decreasing Dreadful/
        Fierce/Swift/Fixed. (Challenging, even difficult times can be used
        to make breakthroughs and to tackle difficult issues head on.)

12   Supportive-Increasing-Fixed

13   Supportive-Decreasing-Swift/Fierce

14   Challenging/Supportive, Increasing/Decreasing, Swift/Fierce

15   Supportive-Increasing-Fixed

Travel is one activity that helps us observe the quality of time in action for a number of reasons. The first is that the results of our action is nearly immediate – we have to deal with the conditions of the quality of time as soon as we leave the house to get into the car or onto the plane or train. Also, when travelling we are thrown into a busy, high-energy, fast-paced environment, such as an airport. In this environment there are many people and conditions which are also affected by the time quality. In this condition of being in transit – destabilized – everyone around us is put into a more susceptible, sensitive and heightened state of awareness, so it is easier to observe the subtlety of time and its effects.

While experimentation and observation will help you discover how time has quality, unless you are recklessly adventurous it is sensible to avoid leaving for long journeys or important trips during a Challenging-Decreasing/Increasing-Dreadful time, as it can disrupt travel plans.

IT'S
ABOUT ACTION
AND OUTCOME

You were born to win, but to be a winner you must plan to win, prepare to win, and expect to win.

Zig Ziglar

The purpose in Panchang is not to try and create a 'perfect' life by navigating around obstacles. Not only is this not possible, but it's foolish to adopt an avoidance approach in that it will limit our growth and our chance to gain knowledge, strength and wisdom.

Panchang is about planting seeds and bringing them to fruition. It's a system that helps us to use the power of time to energize our actions. Although this will lead to experience, it is not so much about **experience** as it is about **outcome**.

For instance there will be times when you have to act and the best that is on offer is a Supportive-Decreasing-Fierce time quality. While such a time will be likely to have its challenging elements, if you harness it effectively, then in due course there is every chance that your actions will have positive results. A challenging experience, for example, could in time develop into a positive situation.

Panchang is a strategic planning tool. It's not as much about dealing with today as about creating tomorrow.

using time quality to your advantage

KNOWING WHEN TO ACT

Opportunity is missed by most people because it is dressed in overalls and looks like work. Thomas Edison

Getting your timing right means getting better results. And the trick of good timing is knowing when the right time arrives. Panchang gives us the signals and this is a huge advantage. As Orson Welles said, 'The one-eyed man is king in the country of the blind'. Interestingly, one of the Sanskrit names for Vedic astrology is **Jyotish**, meaning 'light' or 'the ability to see things clearly now, in the past and in the future'.

Panchang astrology gives us a way to recognize the patterns of time quality and how they influence or symbolize events in the mundane environment. Historians, economists and scientists all plot occurrences with the aim of understanding the patterns they create. Stock traders use financial graphs to plot a trend as a matter of course. Banks analyse financial trends to set interest rates. Monarchs and leaders have always had recourse to astrology and have used it to their advantage, from the **Bhagavad Gita**'s Sri Arjuna on the battlefield of Kurukshetra nearly 5,000 years ago right up to François Mitterrand and Ronald Reagan in the 1980s.

Millionaires don't use astrology, Billionaires do.

J. P. Morgan

Knowledge of Panchang timing saves time, effort and resources because once we recognize the patterns of influence in our environment, we can plan accordingly. So Panchang helps us formulate effective action and over a period of time its use gives us a real advantage.

Time management systems tell us to focus on what is important. They also tell us how to be organized, how to do more in less time. They make suggestions based on managing time quantitatively not qualitatively. Good sense tells us that we have to do both. We have to think of what is important to us – what sort of life we want to work towards – and then manage our time practically to do whatever we need to reach our goals.

Panchang brings a new dimension to time management. It tells us that time can work for us, not against us – that it can be a resourceful ally, not a thief or an adversary. Panchang helps us be flexible, to tune in to our intuition through the din of the everyday world we live in. It values a P-time approach to life and helps us put to one side the M-time conditioning that can hinder our potential. My tendency may be to say, 'Oh I have to do this now!' but Panchang may show me that by waiting for the right time I will avoid unnecessary complications and get better results.

When an idea bubbles to the surface, Panchang either says, 'Yes, you are on the right track' or 'Wait another day or two before you act on this'. What greater advantage is there?

IMPROVE YOUR VISION BEFOREHAND

The beauty of the past is that it is the past. The beauty of the now is to know it. The beauty of the future is to see where one is going.

Hindsight is 20/20. We know what has passed. It is easy to look back and see things for what they are, though even that does not always work, as it may depend on how far back we are looking. In one sense, the greater the distance in time, the better our perspective. Patterns emerge. We understand ourselves better. And the more we understand ourselves, the more we understand events in our lives. The best knowledge is self-knowledge, and hindsight can be helpful in achieving this, as long as we are honest in looking back.

The future is less certain. We feel there are no patterns there for us to recognize and at the deepest level our survival instincts are based on recognizing patterns, on piecing together the conditions into which we are moving. We need some patterns to base our decisions on. So we make plans based on our understanding of the past.

Panchang astrology provides us with a pattern for the future, one that has been tested over thousands of years. Nothing is infallible, of course. But as one English astrologer once remarked, in what profession can you find perfection? Do doctors, lawyers or scientists not make mistakes?

By offering a way to recognize the patterns of time in advance, Panchang gives us 20/20 vision of the future. While there are no guarantees as to **how** the energy of time will manifest in the mundane world, what is true is that the qualities will have their influence.

As you become familiar with Panchang you will be able to see how its language and symbolism manifest in your own life. Language is personal, as are all symbolic systems, and even in the most objective sense is subject to interpretation. The symbolism of Panchang will help you recognize the patterns of time in your own way. Observe how they work on a daily basis and you will learn to judge how they will manifest in the future.

SURF THE WAVES OF TIME

If we keep doing what we're doing, we're going to keep getting what we're getting. Stephen R. Covey

Cycles Mean Change and Change Means Growth

We can recognize patterns because life moves in cycles. Cycles are based on change and yet at the same time they can work to create continuity. Cycles in time help create a certainty and a stable basis. Harnessed in the right way, they can help our growth and make us strong. The trick is in knowing which cycles are valuable and worth repeating, and which are ineffective and worth changing.

Change in itself almost always evokes a sense of fear or dread. Even the most adventurous and restless characters will find it unsettling as well as exhilarating. Our attitude towards change usually determines how effectively we can manage it. Can we muster up the courage to embrace it and use it, grow from it, become wise as a result of it? Or do we shy away from it and think that it is safer to dig in our heels and stick with what we know? At some point in our growth we usually recognize that the known can be a trap or a rut, at which point it becomes even more limiting than the unknown. In order to make the best of ourselves, we should face up to the unknown.

No matter what our attitude towards change, it is always reassuring to have a map. Even if a journey into the unknown is scary or difficult, a map gives us a sense of direction. Panchang can provide one. It can help you to recognize the cycles in your own life. And once you recognize your own life cycles, you can anticipate change and opportunity and be ready to move with the momentum of time.

Everyone thinks of changing the world, but no one thinks of changing himself. Tolstoy

Catch the Wave at the Right Time

The cosmos is a vast living body, of which we are
still parts. The sun is a great heart whose tremors
run through our smallest veins. The moon is a great
nerve-centre from which we quiver for ever. Who
knows the power that Saturn has over us, or Venus?
But it is a vital power, rippling exquisitely through us
all the time. D. H. Lawrence, *Apocalypse*

Time cycles can be seen as waves. The major cycles of a person's life,
called **Dasas** in Sanskrit, which vary in length from seven to 20 years,
can be pictured like the waveforms on an oscilloscope. They begin
slowly at the base and gradually grow in intensity towards the tip, then
slowly lessen in strength on the way down to the nadir which marks the
end of one cycle and the beginning of another. Each of these waves
of energy has sub-levels of energy or influence which can be divided
into finer and finer periods of time. All qualitative time cycles work as
waves of varying strengths, lengths and intensity. The growing phases
of the Moon work in this way, with the greatest energy culminating
towards the Full Moon.

A ship in harbour is safe, but that is not what ships
are built for. William Shed

To exist is to change, to change is to mature, to mature is to go on creating oneself endlessly.

Henri Bergson

Get your Timing Right — Recognizing Patterns

If you can spot a pattern, you are sitting on opportunity. But you have to understand it too. That allows you to plan ahead.

For instance, we all notice economic cycles at work around us: boom-bust cycles, interest rate cycles, cycles in business confidence, cycles in the stock market, commodity price cycles (the value of sugar, zinc, gold, etc). If you wanted to invest in those cycles but didn't understand the pattern, you would have to rely on guesswork. It is recognizing the pattern and understanding how it works that leads to good timing.

Catching the energy of these time cycles can be likened to a surfer catching an ocean wave. The surfer waits for the right moment to begin paddling so as to catch the momentum of the wave and be carried to the shore. In the same way, if you catch the quality of time by acting at the right moment, its energy will carry your action to its destination (not necessarily your goal, but its destination).

If you miss the right moment to act, don't react by rushing to catch up, forcing your actions to begin at the wrong time. Simply wait for the next good wave to come along to begin your action. Because nature works in cycles, a suitably good time will come again, usually fairly soon.

Time and tide wait for no man, but they do return.

By being **passively active**, or **actively passive,** we combine a receptive awareness and reflective response with a dynamic ability to make things happen. With this as a guiding principle it is easier to take advantage of the flow of time-quality cycles so that you can use them effectively. Panchang helps you know when to wait, when to recharge your energies, when to prepare and when to take the right action for any particular cycle of time.

HARMONIOUS ACTION CREATES POSITIVE OUTCOMES

Anything that is wasted effort represents wasted time. The best management of our time thus becomes linked inseparably with the best utilization of our efforts. Ted W. Engstrom

Harmony generates harmony. This is the ripple effect – harmonious action creates positive reaction. Working with the harmony of time means working with the harmony that exists in nature and this helps create prosperity and abundance.

Making an effort to work in harmony with time can also help us learn to work in harmony with ourselves. An act against the natural order is an act against our own self-interest, even if we do not recollect the cause of the reaction when it comes to us. But being conscious of how we create our own obstacles is a source of real freedom.

Working in harmony with time means we are the cause of less friction in our environment. For instance forcing decisions without the backing of your team can lead to friction and misunderstandings, maybe even more problems than the one you were initially trying to solve.

Working with the harmony of time means choosing a good time for creative planning and discussion. Stable times are good for implementing plans and Challenging or Fierce times are good for solving problems.

Being in the flow of time and nature is healthier all round. It creates fewer obstacles. It creates more freedom. There is a cumulative effect – we build a positive momentum in our lives. We may not be able to remove the drag of all our previous ill-judged or badly-timed actions immediately. We all have to accept limits. But with harmonious action the trend is towards a greater freedom.

In India you will see young children playing with a bicycle wheel, rolling it down the road, tapping it with a stick. It is easier to change the direction of the wheel with little taps. Similarly, through harmonious action we gradually create a new and positive direction for our lives.

Astrology does not offer an explanation of the laws of the universe, nor why the universe exists. What it does, to put it in simplest terms, is to show us that there is a rhythm to the universe, and that man's own life partakes of this rhythm. Henry Miller

Knowing how we function as a part of nature is a powerful awareness and brings us closer to a divine understanding of life. The Native Americans understood nature as something which fed and nourished their lives, and honoured the gifts of Mother Earth and Grandfather Sky. In fact most traditional wisdom stresses the importance of working in harmony with nature and not against it. To some extent we have lost the power of that vision. In the long run, it will be important to make that connection again. Being conscious of time quality gives us a holistic view that highlights the connection between everything and suggests that a sense of responsibility towards the general environment is essential if we are not to leave our grandchildren with polluted seas, soil and air.

HAVE A CLEAR IDEA OF WHAT YOU WANT TO DO

Without goals, and plans to reach them, you are like a ship that has set sail with no destination.

Fizhugh Dodson

This seems so obvious. But often in life the most obvious things are the ones we overlook. In practice, deciding upon your direction may be one of your most difficult challenges. And it doesn't happen just once, when we leave school or take our first job. We have to make choices every day.

Vision is everything. Even if it is wrong, it is better to have one than not. It is easier to change direction than to start from a dead stop.

So, create a mental map of your journey. Visualize your destination. Everything begins in consciousness. Notice I didn't say 'mind'. The mind is a fickle thing. By 'consciousness' I mean your being. Your inner self. The soul that is served by your mind, intelligence and senses. The whole you.

Once you have decided where you are going, act with the end in mind, but be ready for a change of plan. Every journey has its detours. Being open to these means being receptive to the higher guidance that comes from within. Being flexible means being humble, having a sense of a higher hand at work that, in seen and unseen ways, moves you along in the right direction, even if it is not towards a destination you originally had in mind.

Acting at the right time is not a guarantee of an easy or straight-forward journey. It can be demanding and ask for a little patience, humility, service – whatever we can offer. But in the end it's the journey that counts. And by acting, with intent, at a harmonious time, you will discover a life less ordinary.

What comes first, the compass or the clock? Before one can truly manage time (the clock), it is important to know where you are going, what your priorities and goals are, in which direction you are headed (the compass). Where you are headed is more important than how fast you are going. Rather than always focusing on what's urgent, learn to focus on what is really important.

BE FLEXIBLE,
BE PATIENT

Instead of thinking about where you are, think about where you want to be. It takes twenty years of hard work to become an overnight success. Diana Rankin

Patience is a rare commodity in a world driven by speed and the demand for immediate gratification. The value of a product or service is often rated on how quickly we can get it and consume it. This value system contradicts the way of the natural world. While advertising claims that we can have it all now, everything takes time and energy to develop and anything of value usually takes a good deal of time. Everything – without exception – has its own natural clock, its own sense of timing, and no amount of rushing or urgency can force something which is not ready. This is especially true of people.

Waiting for our efforts to bear fruit may be a challenge, but most successful people know that the right timing is the magic ingredient of real progress. Successful business people, for example, often say they saw 'a gap in the market', or that their product was 'timely', or simply that they were 'in the right place at the right time'. Good gardeners know that they need to wait for the right season for the flowers or fruit. An apple tree has no leaves in midwinter, but come autumn it will produce a juicy crop. Allowing events to unfold in their own time is not only calming, but enlightening in a most wondrous way.

There came a time when the risk it took to remain tight in the bud was more painful than the risk it took to blossom. Anaïs Nin

However, there is more to the dynamic of action and outcome than timing. We can plan our actions to coincide with auspicious times, but even with our best efforts, good timing and best of intentions, our goal may elude us, take longer than we planned or be realized in an unexpected way. However, working with time, in conjunction with other forms of self-awareness, will give us what we really need for our growth. Being able to read the deeper meaning of life's events opens the door to this exceptional wisdom.

GOOD TIMING
CAN MAKE
EVEN THE HARD
TIMES EASIER

Try not to become a man of success but rather to become a man of value. Einstein

Fortune can be fleeting, but value of character is abiding. Real success lies in the art of living – and being. In good times or in bad, the best company is one's own sense of worth, higher principles and integrity. Success based on these tends to be lasting – even against a backdrop of fluctuating fortunes.

Not only does fortune have its cycles, but people do as well. We all have our ups and downs from time to time. Some of these last a long time, some pass quickly. Vedic astrologers use the **Dasa** system of life cycles and phases which we mentioned earlier (see p. 147) to plot these cycles. This can give enormous value in terms of understanding what influences are at work in our lives and for how long – especially as they are so accurate.

Whether we are in a good period or a challenging one, using the quality of time can improve the overall quality of our position. While acting at the right time will not completely alter difficult conditions, it will steer our actions toward a better outcome. More importantly, it will gradually help us harmonize the quality of our lives so that they are natural – and sublime. The long-term effects of this are immense. They move us towards the most integrated and natural consciousness that we are capable of.

Also, in difficult times we tend to have less energy and fewer resources at our disposal, and good timing can help us make the most of what we have. As mentioned earlier, good timing helps reduce the friction of the results of our previous disharmonious action. And when it is used for charitable efforts, their benefits tend to accrue more quickly, both to us and to others. The right timing lets us make the very most of the good periods and helps us through the bad.

GOOD TIMING
TAKES FOCUS
AND EFFORT

The winds and waves are always on the side of the
ablest navigators. Edward Gibbon

Good timing is not a magic bullet that solves all of life's problems. It
is a tool that can help you make more of life, but it does not **guarantee**
success. To use the quality of time effectively means to be conscious,
diligent, determined and patient and to do the things you are best at.
It means using one more of nature's energies to help you navigate a
sensible and prosperous course through life.

Catching a wave at the right time still requires that you know how to
surf. Otherwise you can end up head first in the sand.

Anyone who has never made a mistake has never
tried anything new. Einstein

Starting at the right time means planting at the right time. Then you have to wait. The seed has to germinate, sprout, break the surface, grow, leaf and flower before it can bear its fruit. It takes time and there will always be challenges to its growth. A stable time offers a solid platform for growth and provides a basis for weathering the difficult winds that are certain to come. So it is best to have an attitude of watchful diligence based on the security of being well prepared and acting at the right time. It also helps to remain flexible, so that when challenges arise you can navigate around them. This practical approach gives the best results in the long run.

DON'T BE FOOLED
BY THE MOOD
OF THE DAY...

A certain amount of opposition is a great help to a man. Kites rise against, not with, the wind. John Neal

Panchang is more about taking action to produce results than about simply monitoring your experience of other people's moods. This is important because the nature of any time can be misleading. For instance we may feel that a Supportive-Increasing-Dreadful time is a little too intense for our liking. Maybe by nature we prefer a Tender or Light quality; it is certainly more pleasant. But we are after results, not simply the transient pleasure of the moment, and it is interesting to note that nearly all the Dreadful time qualities are ruled by the benefic planets Jupiter and Venus and give fast results. So, while a momentary experience may be turbulent and even challenging, the results may be just what we were looking for.

This is very instructive, both philosophically and practically. The hard times give good results, whereas the easy times may not give us, at least in the short term, the blessings we want. So it pays to be strong, to take on a challenge and to be open to life's opportunity when it comes dressed in overalls and looking like hard work! 'Negative' energy can be very creative, whereas 'positive' times may be just **too** nice, giving a false sense of well-being and leading to inertia. It's a matter of outlook and orientation. At the right moment, putting in the effort and facing things head on will, in the long run, bring good results.

This may help us if we are concerned about a time quality that is coming up. Is a Dreadful time going to be 'really dreadful'? How fierce is Fierce likely to be? Using Panchang requires an open mind, a mood to explore, a sense of wonder about the magic of nature, a measure of courage, a touch of wisdom and a good amount of faith in the natural, divine and inherently benevolent aspect of a higher Hand at work. That is a safe place to operate from, and doing so helps us keep things in perspective.

Another point about courage – some people say, 'I would rather not know,' which is too bad, because there is no safety in ignorance. Ignorance is not bliss. While what we do not understand can create fear, it can also inspire inquiry. Stepping over the threshold of fear, we usually ask ourselves how we have lived without the knowledge and wisdom we find. So when in doubt, face the uncertainty. Using uncomfortable times skilfully can bring good results.

experience
the
quality
of
time

SOMETIMES IT'S OBVIOUS, SOMETIMES IT'S SUBTLE

Panchang is subtle and is about subtle parts of life. Knowledge of Panchang is esoteric, meaning 'hidden' or 'mysterious'. It has been hidden to the West because the idea of time having quality begs many philosophical questions. But the truth will out, and by various paths, whether physics or the wisdom traditions of ancient cultures, people are beginning to view time in this way.

Subtle knowledge requires an acute awareness. It demands keen observation and to some extent a mind that enjoys detecting the connections between everything around us. Do we see a cluster of events in our day that tells us something of the quality of time? Does our environment 'talk' to us in a way that gives us a clue to what is really happening?

Someone asked me once if I would teach Panchang, to which I said I would if the student had an interest in art, philosophy, poetry, symbolism, psychology and reading detective novels. Why detective novels? Because a Conan Doyle novel shows in so many ways how appearances are deceiving and how what lies at the root of an event is most often elusive to the casual observer.

For instance does the weather create bad moods? For those of us who live in cloudy England the answer is probably yes, for those who live in sunny California the answer is probably no. But how is the weather connected to our emotional well-being? How do you make the link? Of course we all know that the weather does create our moods, but we may not want to admit it. The weather **itself** does not make things happen – did the hot, muggy weather start the argument with a grumpy taxi driver? Well no, but somewhere down the line it may have had a hand in creating the conditions that resulted in an overheated row.

Most of us do have an awareness that allows us to make these links. We just need to trust it more. We need to listen to our deeper percep-tions. It's a question of consciousness. The mind of a child **sees every-thing**. It has no filter, it's all magic. To the child fantasy is real life – or rather, real life is fantasy. Reconnecting with something of this inno-cence opens the doors of our perception. We see what is happening in a new and exciting way.

TIME
AND
AWARENESS

The struggle of the male to learn to listen to and respect his own intuitive, inner prompting is the greatest challenge of all. His conditioning has been so powerful that it has all but destroyed his ability to be self-aware. Herb Goldberg

A first visit to an astrologer is very interesting, especially if they follow the prescribed Vedic Panchang method. When you enter the room the astrologer makes a chart of the moment. Studying the symbolism of the chart, they **will tell you** the reason for your visit and what you should talk about. For years now I have followed this method and it sidesteps the problem often encountered by therapists who discover their client's real problem just as they are about to leave the session. A woman came to see me some time ago. She was the talkative type and immediately launched into the reason for her visit. I made a chart for the time she had arrived and told her there was another reason. When she nodded in agreement, I told her that she had come to me out of guilt arising from a clandestine romantic affair which was causing her confusion and pain, as her husband was a loyal companion. She was surprised to hear my direct assessment, but admitted she had expected something like this so had formulated her question carefully. Composing herself, she confirmed my analysis and we went on to look at the situation more deeply.

Other Vedic and Panchang astrologers I know have many stories like this. 'How does this work?' people will ask. 'How do you know so much from the chart of the moment?' The answer, simple but foreign to the way we normally think, is that everything is connected to everything else.

Vedic astrology describes the universe as a complete and intercon-nected whole, a unified field, an interconnected cosmic body in which all energies interplay in a harmonious fashion. The chart of the moment symbolizes how the energies are interrelating at that time and the symbols of Panchang form the language the astrologer uses to 'describe' the motive, intent and character of the person sitting in front of them.

The ancient alchemist Hermes Trismegistus is purported to have written: 'What is below is like what is above; what is above is like what is below.' By being aware of what is happening above, in the heavens, the astrologer can deduce what is happening below, mirrored on Earth. In a sense the environment talks to the astrologer. It tells me as an astrologer something of the nature of the moment. Even if I have no chart to look at, I can observe the subtle working of events, move-ments, nature and conditions around me in such a way that my field of vision becomes a chart.

The goal, then, is to listen to our inner voice, our intuitive prompting, to the part of ourselves that is really the most powerful, if only because it is the most honest. This self-awareness is the Holy Grail of Panchang. Despite the conditioning that turns us away from listening to our intuition, if we can tune in to it, we can become aware of time and its quality and act accordingly.

LISTEN
TO YOUR
INTUITION

Trust your hunches. They're usually based on facts filed away just below the conscious level.

Dr Joyce Brothers

Good instincts usually tell you what to do before your head has figured it out. Michael Burke

All creatures are born with instinct. Most animals survive because of it. It's a language that tells them how nature is directing them, how they can work in harmony with it. They don't have much choice, because choosing to ignore the message is dangerous. We have instinct too – our natural inclination to protect our own, for instance – but we also have our intuition, an inner voice that guides, inspires and protects us. Often we tend to discount its quiet whisperings in the midst of more pressing demands from business. Its value often goes unnoticed, as though scientific or logical explanations would offer us more security and certainty. We can try to repress it, but because it is an important part of our survival it continues to try and push through to the surface. What if, rather than repress it, we were to welcome it, encourage it, work with it – unleash it? Most of us know, at least theoretically, that this is a surefire way to success. Nearly 90 per cent of successful business people attribute their success to their intuition and natural sense of good timing, while the Vedas talk about the inner voice as the whisper of **Paramatma**, or 'the divine that is in all of us'. Yogis work at developing their consciousness so that they can hear that whisper more clearly. To them it is the voice of divine guidance. We may call it something else or understand it in a different way, but the effect is the same – it helps us piece together the puzzle of our lives and recognize the patterns, both in hindsight and in advance.

Panchang is a tool that helps confirm our intuition. One venture capitalist put it to the test and kept a diary of the nature and quality of every day for a Lunar month. As a businessman he was used to making far-reaching decisions, but he would attribute these to his business acumen rather than his 'intuition'. He then went to **www.panchang.com** to compare the online quality of time reports to his notes. To his surprise there was a startling level of accuracy. More importantly, what he was left with was a sense that on his own he tended to doubt his inner voice, but the information at **www.panchang.com** had validated the advice it offered.

Our intuition is not always validated, of course, and this can make us doubt it. We tend to rely on what we can see or touch and to doubt our feelings. Feelings are not 'manly' – at least not in the movies. How strange, though, that we tend to discount the subtle parts of our lives when so much of life is about the unseen.

It takes practice to develop our intuition and it is important that we do not delude ourselves with feelings that are expressions of our desires or wants. It is important to be able to separate a genuine 'whisper' from those times when we may be fooling ourselves. But by consciously listening and feeling we can learn to hear the true whispers of the inner voice.

Panchang offers one way to validate those whispers. In time and with use it will simply confirm what you 'already know'. That's a nice place to be.

Often you have to rely on intuition. Bill Gates

PANCHANG
CONFIRMS
YOUR INTUITION

Sometimes we listen to our intuition, sometimes we don't. There are many reasons why we don't listen. They all have their justifications, usually good and logical. So when we are learning to trust our intuition it is useful to have something that confirms it, preferably beforehand. Panchang offers this confirmation in many ways.

If we use Panchang to build our awareness, we will naturally sense when time quality is changing. I had a business client who was very logical and needed things to be proven empirically. He read economics at Oxbridge and liked to visualize facts or projections in boxes, graphs or spreadsheets. If he could measure something and see results, his logical mind could accept it. After initial scepticism he tested Panchang to his own satisfaction and then became zealous about it as a business tool, checking the Time Planner for 'green' or 'red' periods and using it as a planning tool in his business for meetings, important actions and sales strategy. Two years later he is proud of the fact that his intuition has developed to the point where he can sense the time quality shifting gears during the day.

Another Oxbridge graduate, a lawyer, was convinced that 'intuition doesn't exist' and 'can't be proven'. Yet he found Panchang's time reports consistently confirmed his hunches and made his decision-making more powerful.

Panchang is not unique in its ability to confirm your intuition, but it is a particularly effective system because it gives us the ability to look ahead and see what the time quality will be like in a week, a month or a year's time. Even the most intuitive of us will be hard pressed to say what a specific day will be like five years from now. But at **www.panchang.com** you can look ahead to any time and place to see what the quality of time will be then. The website has been built for that purpose.

IT'S A JOURNEY –
GROW AS YOU GO

All the flowers of all the tomorrows are in the seeds of today and yesterday. Chinese proverb

Opportunities multiply as they are seized. Sun Tzu

Panchang opens the road to adventure and discovery. It facilitates an exploration of the world that is subtle and powerful, one that gives a special insight and can foster our personal growth. As with every journey, it is best to set out with a mood of optimism. An open mind is more likely to succeed, if only because it is not filled with preconceptions that shut out new thoughts. Scepticism and a questioning mind are useful on the journey. But cynicism blocks potential and can be a very self-negating trait. The sign of genius is to be able to see what has been there all along, but which no one previously noticed. In this an open mind is everything.

Keep a diary of your journey. Note your observations and your progress. Note the moods, nature and events of the day. You can cross-reference these to what the **www.panchang.com** website says in its daily 'Quality of Time' reports. With practice you will begin to see the patterns emerging. Even if you do not use the website, taking the view that time has quality will gradually help you build an awareness of it. If all you do is look up at the Moon, note whether it is waxing or waning and compare that to how the day feels, that alone may be enough for you to build your own symbolism of time quality.

Give it a try

☾ **Put it to the test.**

Like our venture capitalist, you may choose to put Panchang to the test by keeping a diary of your daily experiences and later comparing it to the information on the online Panchang Time Planner. He found it 'startlingly accurate'. You may find this 'blindfold' approach is a good first step, or you may want to look up the information on www.panchang.com first and then compare it to your own daily observations.

☾ **Be observant.**

You may need to increase your powers of patience, observation and perception. As you do this you will find you don't jump to conclusions so much and are less swayed by events, so that you can develop a more strategic view of time.

☾ **Try to be patient.**

Try this out. When you are experiencing a chaotic, disruptive time, rather than reacting to events, take a step back. Make a deliberate decision to bide your time and wait for a more constructive moment to act, knowing that by doing so you will avoid creating more confusion or complications. Later look back on the event and its outcome and see if it worked. This will help with making important decisions and dealing with difficult situations.

☾ **The varieties of time quality are endless.**

Although we have illustrated 11 major categories, these mix with many other astrological conditions to create unique moments that will not be precisely replicated for another 25,000 years – and even then the epoch will colour the expression of the quality and give it new meaning. The best way to understand time quality is to be aware of it, use it, experiment with it, explore it and discover its unique expression in your own life.

fundamentals

DO WHAT
YOU'RE GOOD AT

Make no little plans. They have no magic to stir men's blood and probably themselves will not be realized. Make big plans. Aim high in hope and work. Remembering that a noble, logical diagram once recorded will not die.   Daniel H. Burnham

Do what you love for a living, and you'll never work another day in your life.   Kung Fu Tse (Confucius)

The quote from Confucius says it all. It tells us that when we are not being who we are, or were born to be, that life is hard work. When we find our true calling, life is a gift. Each one of us has a special nature, a set of unique qualities that, given a chance to express themselves, will bring something to the world and fulfilment to ourselves.

But being ourselves is not easy. To many of us, life seems a conspiracy to deny us the pleasure of knowing who and what we really are. It starts early in life, in small compromises that we make to get along, to fit in, to be accepted. Mostly the compromises seem innocent enough, but gradually our sense of self is worn away and often we are left to quietly mourn that loss alone or to dull it with distraction and entertainment. Such a loss is not only a shame but a forfeit of all that we are. Imagine how much this potential represents to our individual and collective benefit. Imagine what could happen if just a part of it were set free.

When I think of the famous statistic that we only use 10 per cent of our brain I think of it in another way – that we are only using 10 per cent of ourselves, of our deeper personality and potential. It's not really about our brain, but about ourselves.

Reclaiming the 90 per cent is not easy. There is our conditioning to deal with, people's expectations of who we **should** be, our own sense of uncertainty about who we are. But the potential rewards are too significant to not take a step, any step, no matter how tentative, towards becoming our real selves. In the **Bhagavad Gita** Sri Krishna tells Arjuna that it's 'better to fail in doing **your** work than to unnaturally do the work of another'. There is a lot of meaning in this statement, including the fairly basic but important idea that it is better to be honest to your own nature. This simple idea lies at the core of real personal power.

A vision without a task is but a dream. A task without a vision is drudgery. A vision with a task is the hope of the world. Anonymous

Doing a job, no matter how 'simple', that suits your personality is better than going against your nature for the promise of gain. In your true vocation you will find your work a vehicle for self-expression and for relating with people, and you will be more yourself, interact with people more effectively and be more creative. At the heart of most successes is a love of one's work, a natural interest, a passion for what one does. If nothing else this helps one have staying power, patience and determination, which are all important for realizing any goal.

Working in harmony with your nature allows you to realize your potential, to express the best of yourself. Whether it's being a hairdresser, a stockbroker, a painter, a mother or something else entirely, doing what comes naturally to you will help you to do it very well and will bring real rewards.

Vedic astrology gives a deep insight into who you are and what your potential is. If you explore its symbolism you find a way to unfold your potential in ways you previously thought impossible. The **www.panchang.com** website offers a Lunar report, which is a description of your inner nature. The Lunar report is just a fraction, a taste, of what Vedic astrology can offer. To meet a Vedic astrologer and go into your chart in depth can be a special experience that opens many doors. So many times I have heard clients express how for the first time someone really understands them, in a deep way, a way which they don't have to justify.

In a sense Vedic astrology offers a manual, a guidebook, that can help us overcome the conditioning imposed by our environment. It can point us in the direction of our natural self. Panchang reveals our natural talents and the potential we are born with, as well as how we can bring out the best of this potential. It also helps us have realistic expectations. It can set us off on a new journey in search of our lost self, the person we know is in us but which has yet to fully blossom.

Rather than trying to get a lot out of time by playing the wrong role, if you are playing the right one, your natural intuition and purpose can relate to the nature of the moment. Time then carries you along to real fulfilment.

To thine own self be true.   William Shakespeare

Think about it

Everyone has natural talent and purpose. Find yours and be fulfilled. It's all about knowing who you are, **being confident** about who you are and dedicating yourself to what you are really good at.

Give it a try

☽ Think back to your childhood. What did you want to be when you grew up? Is that ludicrous now? Why?

☽ Are you doing what you really want to do, expressing your true potential through your work and daily activities?

☽ What is your dream job?

Find the seed at the bottom of your heart and bring forth a flower. Shigenori Kameoka

DO MORE
IN LESS TIME

The only reason for time is so that everything doesn't happen at once. Einstein

The greatest wastes are unused talents and untried ideas. Anonymous

To be productive and stay healthy, we need to reach a happy balance in our life – and that means building a good balance of work, relaxation, recreation and meditation into our lifestyle. If you look at the range of time qualities and what they represent, you will see that there is a time for action: Fierce, Increasing; a time for passion: Tender, Supportive; a time for being busy: Swift, Supportive; a time for playful recreation: Light, Supportive; a time for rest and relaxation: Tender, Decreasing; and a time for creativity and inspiration: Light or Tender. These examples are not comprehensive, but they show the flow of time and the organic regulation it brings.

The balance that we need in our life is intrinsic to the natural cycles of time in a week, month or year. Nature Herself helps us by building into

Her cycles the natural qualities that help regulate the flow of events and conditions around us – regardless of whether we perceive them or not.

A balanced approach to time helps us 'create' more time because we are spending the right amount of effort and energy on the right things. That means effective use of energy. It helps us make the most of what time we have and what we are.

Time is the element in which we exist....We are either borne along by it or drowned in it.

Joyce Carol Oates, **Marya**

Do what you're good at and your work can be an expression of your life purpose. It can give you a sense of achievement and satisfaction.

Keep a sense of playfulness and enjoyment in your life to awaken your imagination and creative problem-solving and give yourself a sense of **joie de vivre**.

Learn to relax. It will help you to stay focused, be physically and emotionally healthy, rise above stress and recharge your energy levels. Make space to daydream, still your mind or meditate. It will refresh your vision, give you a sense of perspective, a sense of detachment from daily hassles, remind you of your place in the bigger picture and reconnect you to your source of inspiration.

We have to step outside the daily round from time to time to get in touch with who we really are. It helps us connect with our source of inspiration, which lies outside the confines of the space-time continuum. That's when we glimpse our highest potential and have our most inspired ideas.

Give it a try

☾ Try taking a freer, more natural approach to managing your time, one that is less focused on doing and more focused on being. Of course you will have to do what's necessary in your day, but take a moment now and then to switch off your mind, reconnect your spirit and be conscious of being in the flow of natural time.

TIME FOR
RELATIONSHIPS

Everything is determined, the beginning as well as
the end, by forces over which we have no control. It
is determined for the insect as well as for the star.
Human beings, vegetables, or cosmic dust, we all
dance to a mysterious tune, intoned in the distance
by an invisible piper.[8] Einstein

There may be no field of experience in which time plays so influential
and obvious a role as relationships. There are so many factors that
influence relationships, not least of which are our basic characters.
From an astrological point of view we all have unique traits that make
us special. It takes 25,000 years for the planets to come back to
the same configuration they were in at your birth. Even when they do
return, the larger-scale time periods will have changed, thus modifying
the conditions. It has long been argued by psychologists, and now
geneticists, whether our characters are down to 'nature or nurture'.
Are we born with a built-in nature or are we formed by the influences
and experience of our environment? The Panchang view is that it is
both, with an emphasis on nature, modified by experience and influenced by the quality of time.

We express our natures in our relationships – not just romantic relationships, but all our dealings with others. Exchanges and events
shape them, help us grow or, in bad cases, stunt our development.
Whether through nature or nurture, the field of relationships is where
we become who and what we are, where we unfold our potential.

Of the many factors that influence relationships, from a Panchang
viewpoint the predominant ones include the characters of the two
people relating, how their natures complement or conflict with each
other, the dynamics of harmony (or disharmony) of the two charts, and
the nature and quality of the time of interaction.

Challenges in relationships usually come from misunderstandings –
not having a complete picture of the other person, not realizing what
makes them tick. They may act in a way that gives us one impression,
but deep down they may be motivated by something very different.
Once we know what is happening, though, we can find acceptance
and a greater ability to work with what we have in a relationship. We
know where we stand and this, more than anything else, is essential to
healthy interaction. We may not like certain traits in another person,
but because we understand them, they challenge us less and create
less fear and uncertainty for us.

Panchang astrology can give us an overview of the character of a
person – how they look at the world, how they communicate (or don't),
how they interact with others, their fears, hopes and desires – and can
show us how we can interact with them in a way that works for
both of us. We will open the door to this subject in a future book, but
for now it is important to understand something of the dynamic of
Panchang astrology in relationships.

One of the biggest but most subtle of influences on relationships can be the quality of time. How is it, for instance, that we can be in a perfectly happy and contented relationship, and for no explainable reason a row erupts over something trivial? There are many different explanations and influences – some whose cause is immediate and visible, others whose cause is more remote and hidden. Maybe the two people involved are feeling on edge, tense and nervous, but what is influential in creating those issues and bringing them to a head is the quality of time.

If you knew that the time quality was unstable, chaotic, disruptive and discordant, would you have an important discussion, especially one of a sensitive nature?

Even where we have strong and abiding relationships based on long-established trust, the quality of time can still affect our interactions. Panchang helps us time our important interactions more effectively to ensure that we get the most from them – and contribute the most to them as well.

How Time is a Healer in our Relationships

Being more aware of the natural flux of time quality can bring greater harmony to your home, family and love life. In situations where we are looking for emotional support or hoping to gain something from someone, perhaps to ask for a pay rise or some form of backing, the time quality can play a positive role in the outcome.

Panchang is as helpful a tool in our personal life as it is in business. It can help us to tend our friendships, family relationships and marriage or close partnerships. Some times are especially supportive for close relationships and offer a nurturing, stable basis for commitment. Equally, disharmonious or unstable times can, if we are unconscious of them, destroy or undermine a relationship.

A turbulent time quality can, however, be helpful in bringing matters to a head. There are times when the only way forward is to raise diffi-cult issues. Yet it's not always helpful to try to resolve matters at a harsh and unstable time. It can end up being even more destructive all round. It makes sense to discuss making long-term improvements or life-changing decisions at a more calm and supportive time.

If we can harmonize our exchanges with the quality of time, we will find that this quite naturally helps relationships flow and that we understand each other better.

Use soft words and hard arguments. English proverb

Don't Take Things Personally

Sometimes the time quality is particularly sharp and someone we were hoping would be supportive seems too stressed to deal with us sensitively. Similarly, there are other occasions when we are under stress ourselves and may say hurtful things in the heat of the moment.

If you are feeling stressed it is worth bearing in mind that those around you are likely to be feeling the pinch from the challenging conditions too. Any harsh words from them could just be a reflection of the moment. The time quality may even be **exaggerating** the experience. Stepping back and realizing there is a harsh quality of time at work enables us to take things less personally and to make a more measured response, so that we avoid adding more tension that will only make matters worse. If we then want to take matters further, we can wait for a time that is more supportive to discussion. In this way Panchang helps us put things in perspective.

Pick your Moment

When I am working on a problem I never think about beauty. I only think about how to solve the problem. But when I have finished, if the solution is not beautiful, I know it is wrong. Buckminster Fuller

Personal time is precious. In our culture it is becoming increasingly rare, busy as we are with work and other commitments. So it is more important than ever to ensure that whatever time we have for friendships and relationships is **quality time**, time that is supportive and nurturing and that makes a difference.

We usually take great care to select the right place for an important romantic date. It makes equally good sense to pick the right time. A Tender time can enhance a loving mood, while a Light time quality will help to create a bright and breezy atmosphere for socializing.

Panchang can also help you avoid stressful times. There is nothing worse than bringing a sense of urgency into a romantic setting. It creates stress, tension and awkwardness. If you know the quality of time is abrasive, you can anticipate that people may be touchy or argumentative and this can help you avoid disappointment – and even create understanding and empathy in a discordant environment.

Sometimes tensions get the better of us and a row develops. Luckily you can also use Panchang to find the right quality of time for making up after an argument. A harmonious time can help you reach agreement after any discord.

Sometimes we can end up having a row because we have been affected by the time quality without knowing it. If this has happened you can check the **www.panchang.com** Time Planner for clues about the quality of time during the row. This can help keep things in perspective and may also offer an insight into the deeper issues at work.

Panchang can be your early warning system, helping you navigate the problem times as well as enjoy the good times to the full.

He who every morning plans the transaction of the day and follows out that plan carries a thread that will guide him through the labyrinth of the most busy life. ...But where no plan is laid, where the disposal of time is surrendered merely to the chance of incidents, chaos will soon reign. Victor Hugo

Give it a try

We are all used to picking a mutually convenient place and time for important business meetings. Panchang can also help us pick our moments to create the right atmosphere for our personal relationships. You may want to choose the time carefully to:

☽ get engaged

☽ tell someone you're pregnant

☽ start trying to conceive

☽ let your partner know you're having an affair

☽ split up decisively but without acrimony

☾ ask someone out for a first date

☾ go out for a romantic meal

☾ go away together

☾ have a family get-together

☾ entertain friends

8   Ronald W. Clark, *Einstein: The Life and Times,* Sceptre, 1996, p. 422.

what
to
expect

WELL-TIMED RESULTS

You are never given a wish without also being given the power to make it come true. You may have to work for it, however. Richard Bach, *Illusions*

Panchang is about practical results. It is about value for time. It opens up an awareness that many ancient cultures had about time, one that emphasizes our relationship to nature, our being part of nature. Panchang is about using time in subtle, conscious and effective ways.

If the quality of time is subtle, then in some ways the results of using Panchang are also subtle. But gradually a pattern emerges and we begin to understand the connections between everything around us and everyone around us. The sublime becomes commonplace and normal life takes on an unexpected magical element.

Panchang is a tool, not a belief system, but it helps us understand the wisdom of the ancient sages, no matter what tradition they hailed from. It connects us to a wisdom that affirms our efforts **to be** and become ourselves. It gives a sense of wonder, asks many questions and inspires us to journey toward a harmony with ourselves, with others and our environment. It may help us see that our world is crying out for a different way of doing things. In a small but potent way, Panchang can help us find that way, one that will give us better results – for ourselves and for the world around us.

The world is round and the place which may seem like the end may also be the beginning. Ivy Baker Priest

www.panchang.com

That we can now think of no mechanism for astrology is relevant but unconvincing. No mechanism was known, for example, for continental drift when it was proposed by Wegener. Nevertheless, we see that Wegener was right, and those who objected on the grounds of unavailable mechanism were wrong.

Carl Sagan

The Time Planner

Use It Effectively – Plan Ahead

By now you may want to put Panchang to the test and use it in your daily life. To make this easy for you we have built the website **www.panchang.com**, which has all the tools and information you need. The site is very interactive and invites exploration. It lets you plan your day and any important actions you want to take in the future.

The website represents an historic first in putting powerful astrological decision-making tools into the hands of everyone. With it, you have the chance to look at time in a qualitative way and make well-informed astrologically-supported decisions that are based on both the quality of time in general and your own unique astrological birth chart.

More astonishingly perhaps, the website even offers the opportunity to look into the future to find the best days and times for important actions. It would normally take an astrologer many hours, if not days, to make the calculations and analysis to find these 'Best Times'. Now anyone can instantly explore the future and plan hundreds of activities, from Business to Romance, Leisure to Education, Home to Travel, and many more, like 'Starting a Business', 'Selling a House', 'Getting Married', 'Revising and Study', 'Adventure Travel' and 'Home Building'. Your time planning will be revolutionized.

The site has information and help files that let you get right in and use it, but while everything you need is there, it may be helpful to mention some of the main features you will find.

Quality of Time Score

Panchang Ltd has developed a patented scoring system that represents the many thousands of astrological factors that create the quality of time as a simple numeric value system of plus 10 to minus 10. Plus 10 is the most positive, constructive and helpful time and minus 10 the most challenging, unsettled and discordant time. These values are calculated by analysing the general quality of time and then comparing them to the unique conditions of your astrological chart. The number is special to you as an individual and to your location on Earth at any particular time.

Quality of Time Text

Every day has a short but detailed description that tells you the quality and influence of the current period. This report is partly general to the location but it is also personal to you. Knowing the quality of time in advance is a great advantage that can help your planning and also confirm your intuition and hone your perceptive skills.

Time Quality Search Engine

Another **www.panchang.com** first, this powerful search engine searches the future for days and times perfectly suited to you and your location. It presents its findings with amazing speed and calculates the best times for you to do any given activity.

Activity Score

All the activity scores at **www.panchang.com** are astrologically specific to you, the time, your location and the nature of the activity.

Best Times in the Day

This is a feature that is presented on the Panchang daily agenda **(see below)** which presents the best, worst and neutral times of every day as green, red and yellow respectively, following the traffic light metaphor. It's simple, easy to read and powerful. If the day is challenging or unstable, you can use these times to schedule your important actions and avoid the worst of the day's destabilizing influence.

Best Times in the Week

This is a graph of your personal high and low power principles for the week, which enables you to schedule important meetings and plan for your most powerful times.

Location

You can select almost any place on Earth and obtain information on any day and time. Live in London but do business in Hong Kong? Simply add Hong Kong to your list of locations. You can add as many locations as you like and change your location anytime you like. Great for the busy executive, intrepid adventurer or eco-warrior!

Agenda

You can use your agenda to add in appointments according to the day and time information, so that the really important actions in your life are aligned to the quality of time.

'To Do' List

Panchang can notify you by e-mail or SMS text on your mobile phone of your appointments or items on your 'to do' list.

More, Many More and More Coming

The above are just a few of the many features at **www.panchang.com**. There are also personalized Lunar reports that describe your character using Panchang astrology and the groundbreaking Compatibility report that describes how you and your lover, friend or colleague get on will be available soon.

Contact Us for Consultations

The Lunar report, which describes a person's inner nature and potential, is available online at **www.panchang.com** or by mail order from Panchang Ltd, PO Box 2837, Bath, BA1 2FR, UK.

Full chart readings, which map the time periods of an individual's life, as well as their inner nature, public persona, talents, strengths, opportunities, life circumstances and challenges, are available in the form of one-to-one consultations, either by telephone or in person.

BIBLIOGRAPHY

Adam, Barbara, Timewatch: The Social Analysis of Time, Polity Press, 1995

Ariotti, P. E., 'The concept of time in western antiquity', The Study of Time II: Proceedings of the Second Conference of the International Society for the Study of Time, Lake Yamanaka – Japan, eds J. T. Fraser and N. Lawrence, Springer-Verlag, Berlin and New York, 1975

Aventi, Anthony F., Empires of Time: Calendars, Clocks and Cultures, I. B. Tauris, 1990

Bacon, Francis, The Masculine Birth of Time, 1602

Bienfait, H. F., 'Time in Nature' in Time: A Catalogue, ed. A. J. Turner, Foundation of Time for Time, Amsterdam, 1990

Brady, J. Biological Timekeeping, Soc. Exp. Biol. Seminar Series 14, Cambridge University Press, 1982

Campbell, J., Winston Churchill's Afternoon Nap, Simon & Schuster, New York, 1986

Capra, Fritjof, The Tao of Physics, Wildwood House, 1975

Clark, Ronald W., Einstein: The Life and Times, Sceptre, 1996

Climent, C. E., and Plutchik, R., 'Lunar madness: an empirical study', Compr. Psychiatry 18 (4), 1997, 369–74

Cloudsley-Thompson, J. L., 'Biological clocks and their synchronizers', The Study of Time III: Proceedings of the Third Conference of the International Society for the Study of Time, Alpbach – Austria, eds J. T. Fraser, N. Lawrence and D. Park, Springer-Verlag, New York, 1978

— Biological Clocks: Their Function in Nature, Weidenfeld & Nicolson, London, 1980

Coveney, Peter, and Highfield, Roger, The Arrow of Time, introduction by Ilya Prigogine, Flamingo, London, 1991

Cowan, James, Mysteries of the Dream-Time: The Spiritual Life of Australian Aborigines, Prism Press, 1992

Davis, Stan, and Meyer, Christopher, Blur: The Speed of Change in the Connected Economy, Little Brown & Co., 1999

De Quincey, Thomas, Confessions of an Opium Eater and Other Writings, Oxford University Press, 1985

De Vries, Simon John, Yesterday, Today, and Tomorrow: Time and History in the Old Testament, SPCK, London, 1975

Dekker, Elly, 'From a World Ruling Time to a Time-ruled World', Time: A Catalogue, ed. A. J. Turner, Foundation of Time for Time, Amsterdam, 1990

Dijkhuis, Willem, 'A Hinge in Time', Time: A Catalogue, ed. A. J. Turner, Foundation of Time for Time, Amsterdam, 1990

Ditton, J., 'Absent at work; or how to manage monotony', New Society 22, 21 December 1972

BIBLIOGRAPHY

Eliade, Mircea, 'Time and Eternity in Indian Thought', Man and Time, ed. Joseph Campbell, Princeton University Press, 1957

Fisher, Roland, 'Biological Time', Voices of Time, ed. Fraser

Folkard, S., and Monk, T. H., 'The Circadian Performance Rhythms', Hours of Work: Temporal Factors in Working Schedules, eds S. Folkard and T. H. Monk, Wiley, Chichester, England, 1985

Folkard, Simon, and Hunt, L. J., 'Morningness-Eveningness and Long-Term Shiftwork Tolerance', Shiftwork in the 21st Century: Challenges for Research and Practice, Peter Lang

Fox, Robin (ed.), A Research Portfolio on Chronic Fatigue, Royal Society of Medicine Press, 1998

Franklin, Benjamin, Advice to a Young Tradesman, 1748

Fraser, J. T., Lawrence, N., and Haber, F. C. (eds), Time, Science, and Society in China and the West: The Study of Time, University of Massachusetts Press, Amherst, 1986

Gell, Alfred, The Anthropology of Time: Cultural Constructions of Temporal Maps and Images, Berg, Oxford, 1992

Ghazi, Polly, and Jones, Judy, Getting a Life: The Downshifter's Guide to Happier, Simpler Living, Hodder & Stoughton, London, 1997

Ghiandoni, G., Secli, R., Rocchi, M. B., and Ugolini, G., 'Incidence of lunar position in the distribution of deliveries: a statistical analysis', Minerva Ginecol. 49 (3), 1997, 91–4

Girardet, Herbert, Earthrise: Halting the Destruction, Healing the World, Paladin, 1992

Givens, Douglas R., An Analysis of Navajo Temporality, University Press of America, 1977

Gleick, James, Faster, Little, Brown and Company, London, 1999

Gould, Stephen J., Time's Arrow, Time's Cycle: Myth and Metaphor in the Discovery of Geological Time, Penguin, London, 1991

Griffiths, Jay, Pip Pip, Flamingo, London, 1999

Hager, L. Michael, 'The nonstop city', The Futurist, May/June 1997

Halberg, Franz, 'Quo vadis basic and clinical chronobiology: promise for health maintenance', American Journal of Anatomy 168 (543–94), 1983, 569–70

Hall, Edward T., The Dance of Life: The Other Dimension of Time, Anchor Press/Doubleday, 1983

Harding, Michael, 'Astrology: the language of time', Journal of the Society for Existential Analysis Vol. 4

Hoagland, H., 'The physiological control of judgements of duration: evidence for a chemical clock', Journal of General Psychology 9, 1933

Hope, Jenny, and Chapman, James, 'Moonstruck', Daily Mail, 13 December 2000

James, William, The Principles of Psychology, Dover, New York, 1950; first published Henry Holt and Company, 1890

Kleitman, N., 'Studies on the physiology of sleep', American Journal of Physiology 104, 1933

Landes, David, Revolution in Time, Clocks and the Making of the Modern World, Belknap Press,

Harvard University Press, 1983

— The Wealth and Poverty of Nations: Why Some Are So Rich and Some So Poor, W. Norton, New York, 1998

Lane, John, A Snake's Tail Full of Ants: Art, Ecology and Consciousness, Resurgence Books, 1996

Levine, Robert, A Geography of Time, Basic Books, 1998

Lieber, A. L., 'Human aggression and the lunar synodic cycle', J. Clin. Psychiatry 39 (5), 1978, 385–92

Macnaghten, Phil, and Urry, John, 'Nature and Time', Contested Natures, Sage Publications, 1998

Manheim, Ralph (trans.), Man and Time: Papers from the Eranos Yearbooks, Princeton University Press, New York, 1957

Mann, A. T., The Round Art, Dragon's World, Limpsfield, Surrey, 1979

Mbiti, John S., African Religions and Philosophy, Anchor Books/Doubleday, Garden City, New York, 1969

Melbin, M., 'City Rhythms', The Study of Time III: Proceedings of the Third Conference of the International Society for the Study of Time, Alpbach – Austria, eds J. T. Fraser, N. Lawrence and D. Park, Springer-Verlag, New York, 1978

Melbin, Murray, Night as Frontier: Colonizing the World After Dark, Free Press, 1987

Melton, Lisa, 'Rhythm and blues', New Scientist, 3 June 2000

Moore–Ede, Martin C.; Fuller, Frank; Charles A.; Sulzman, M.; The Clocks That Time Us: Physiology of the Circadian Timing System, Harvard University Press, 1990

Narby, Jeremy, The Cosmic Serpent: DNA and the Origins of Knowledge, Victor Gollancz, 1998

Nowotny, H., 'Time Structuring and Time Measurement: On the Interrelation between Timekeepers and Social Time', The Study of Time II: Proceedings of the Second Conference of the International Society for the Study of Time, Lake Yamanaka – Japan, eds J. T. Fraser and N. Lawrence, Springer-Verlag, Berlin and New York, 1975

Oderda, G. M., and Klein-Schwartz, W., 'Lunar cycle and poison centre calls', J. Toxicol. Clin. Toxicol. 20 (5), 1983, 487–95

Palmer, An Introduction to Biological Rhythms, Pergamon, New York, 1974

Panikkar, Raimundo, 'Time and History in the Tradition of India: Kala and Karma', Cultures and Time, eds L. Gandet et al., UNESCO Press, 1976

Peat, F. David, Blackfoot Physics: A Journey into the Native American Universe, Fourth Estate, London, 1995

Perry, Susan, and Dawson, Jim, The Secrets our Body Clocks Reveal, Rawson Associates, New York, 1988

Picardie, J., 'Moon', Bare, November–December 2000, 57–67

Pliny the Elder, Natural History

Poole, Robert, Time's Alteration: Calendar Reform in Early Modern England, London, UCL Press, 1998

Poulet, Georges, Studies in Human Time, John Hopkins Press, 1956

Pritchard, Edward Evan Evans, The Nuer: A Description of the Modes of Livelihood and Political Institutions of a Nilotic People, Clarendon Press, Oxford, 1940

Pritchard, Evan T., No Word for Time: The Way of the Algonquin People, Council Oak Books, 1997

Quinones, Ricardo, The Renaissance Discovery of Time, Harvard University Press, 1972

Raymond, Martin, 'The time machine', Viewpoint 7

Saint-Exupéry, Antoine de, The Little Prince, Heinemann, London, 1944

Spangler, M., 'Time Proverbs and Social Change in Belgrade, Yugoslavia', The Study of Time IV: Papers from the Fourth Conference of the International Society for the Study of Time, Alpbach – Austria, eds J. T. Fraser, N. Lawrence and D. Park, Springer-Verlag, New York, c.1981

Spencer, Neil, 'Stargazers? But of course', Observer, 12 November 2000

Suzuki, Daisetz Teitaro, Zen and Japanese Culture, Routledge & Kegan Paul, London, 1959

Thakur, C. P., Sharma, R. N., and Akhtar, H. S., 'Full moon and poisoning', Br. Med. J. 281, 1980, 1,684

Thompson, E. P., 'Time, work discipline and industrial capitalism', Past and Present 38, December 1967

Turner, A. J., 'The Origins of Modern Time', Time: A Catalogue, ed. A. J. Turner, Foundation of Time for Time, Amsterdam, 1990

'Lunacy revisited: the influence of the moon on mental health and quality of life', Journal of Psychosocial Nursing, May 2000

Van der Post, Laurens, Jung and the Story of our Time, Hogarth Press, 1976

Vance, D. E., 'Belief in lunar effects on human behaviour', Psychol. Rep. 76 (1), 1995, 32–4

Waugh, Alexander, Time: From Micro-seconds to Millennia – The Search for the Right Time, Headline, London, 1999

Whitrow, G. J., What is Time?, Thames and Hudson, London, 1972

Wilkins, Christopher, The Horizontal Instrument, Doubleday, London, 1999

Young, Michael, The Metronomic Society, Thames and Hudson, London, 1988

Zerubavel, Eviatar, Hidden Rhythms: Schedules and Calendars in Social Life, University of Chicago Press, 1981

Zukav, Gary, The Dancing Wu Li Masters, William Morrow, New York, 1979

INDEX